D1065443

A WOMAN'S CHOICE

A
WOMAN'S
CHOICE

...living through your problems

from confusion to peace

by

EUGENIA PRICE

Author of *Woman to Woman*, etc.

ZONDERVAN PUBLISHING HOUSE

GRAND RAPIDS   MICHIGAN

To my loyal and encouraging
friends — the women who dare
to think with me!

PREFACE

I have written this book with one prayer and one wish in my heart: That you who read it will be encouraged to *think*. Too often, we are content to let someone else do our thinking for us. This seems to be particularly true of women. Dr. Mary Bunting, president of Radcliffe College, has had as one of her life themes, the necessity for today's woman to make use of her mind. I do not say that Christian women necessarily think *less* than other women, but I do believe the Christian woman has an added responsibility to God where her mind is concerned. Too often, in an emergency situation, we act as though our faith had nothing whatever to do with the circumstances. I saw a cartoon the other day in which two identical figures stood side by side. The caption read: "Which one is the believer?" The human mind lighted from *within* by the very Presence of the Spirit of God, should be easily recognized by its ability to cope with the problems of life on this earth.

A Woman's Choice is not an intellectual approach to the problems we all face. It is written in "our language," but with the one theme: That if we begin to face the real issues involved, we are merely making creative use of the minds God gave us. The ability to *think through* is one of the means God has given us to find our way to fulfillment on this earthly journey.

Those of you who read my book, *Woman to Woman*, have literally propelled me into this one by your warm enthusiasm and your generous sharing of the good news of your changed lives. *Woman to Woman* was not an easy book to follow, and yet my stimulating contacts with you in person and by mail since its publication, made writing *A Woman's Choice* a *must.* The two books are two sides of the same picture — woman and God and the daily dilemma. If a woman can choose to live her life in a person-to-Person relationship with God, then she must assume the responsibility of using her mind instead of her emotions when the going gets rough. She must be willing to let that mind be in *her,* which was in Christ Jesus.

This is her *choice.* I have attempted to share some light I have received on how to do this in the book you are about to read. We can live *through* our problems, from confusion to peace, or we can bumble along taking the jolts which inevitably follow a life guided only by the often stormy and reckless winds of our emotions. In fact, I have come to believe that we cannot preserve our healthy, constructive emotions unless we do make maximum use of the minds God has given us.

I feel a deep desire to urge you *not* to skip around in this book. (Even the reviewers may have to read most of it, or take a chance on missing my point entirely!) Part One has to do with the *confusion* which inevitably results from the existence of the eight basic problems selected for treatment. These eight problems I chose directly from the situations about which women have spoken or written to me in the years since the publication of *Woman to Woman.* In Part One, we explore these problems rather thoroughly, with numerous illustrations from real life.

If you stop with Part One, however, you will probably feel only despair! So I urge you to read on. Part Two moves toward the positive. The last four chapters are the important chapters in the book. With every line I wrote, I became more and more convinced that we are missing *most* of the potential God offers us for creative living. But creative living is possible, and He is longing to cooperate with us as we sincerely set ourselves to live *through* our problems — and not *under* them.

Once more, my heart wants to thank my Mother and all of you who prayed for me as I wrote. My thanks as usual to Johnny Erickson, who worked fast and interestedly with me on the typescript. And to my dear friend, Joyce Blackburn, I owe an eternal debt of gratitude, not only for her patient reading aloud to me of every chapter as it was written, but for her always perceptive suggestions and criticisms. Because it is so interesting to me that God reveals His truths to us at times through each other, I feel I must tell you that the seed thoughts for the opening revelations of fresh truth which I have incorporated in the important last chapters came to me also through a conversation with her.

My thanks as always to everyone at Zondervan Publishing House, not only for their valued friendship in Christ and their kindness to me, but because once more, for another book, I have had the good freedom to write as I believe God has directed me.

I am grateful, too, for the permission to use excerpts from letters and conversations, without which this book would be just so much theory.

My heart has been much involved with you during the days I was writing *A Woman's Choice*. You will be reading surrounded by my prayers and caring.

Chicago, Illinois   EUGENIA PRICE
July, 1962

Table of Contents

Part One

From Confusion

1: Understanding the Real Issues

1:

UNDERSTANDING THE REAL ISSUES

The nervous young mother snapped and unsnapped the catch on her purse as she talked.

"I try! Honestly, I do try to control my temper with my children. They're not bad youngsters. I think they're probably just normal. I go along for three or four days, mostly being sweet with them and boom! Off I go again."

Then she shut her eyes tightly, squeezing sudden tears down on her cheeks. "Somehow the part that breaks my heart the most is that now I'm beginning to be cross and irritable with my husband! And I'm terribly in love with him — as much as I was when I married him. We always prided ourselves on being just right for each other — what's happening to me? Why doesn't God answer my prayers for a better disposition?"

There was no doubt whatever about the sincerity of this woman's heart and intentions toward her family. She loved her husband and she loved her children. But she was beginning to hate herself, and she carried around a growing load of guilt that only increased her inner turmoil with the passing of every day.

What was her real problem? Was it her disposition? She honestly thought it was. Suddenly, she had turned into a total mystery to herself. Hour after hour she agonized on her knees, begging God to calm her down and make her sweet tempered and confident as she had been in the early years of her marriage. God seemed not to be listening! Why?

He was listening, all right. And with all His great heart of love, He longed to help her live successfully through this current crisis. What was wrong? Obviously, she was making no progress. Obviously, she was not living *through* the trouble toward a peaceful existence again. By her own admission, the situation was growing worse. But she was praying, she was trying! And she was. What else could she do?

She could begin to face the real issue. She could take careful, intelligent stock of the whole matter and discover the *real problem.* Disposition is not always the real *cause* of trouble. Disposition is frequently the *result* of trouble. When she began to think things through, she discovered for herself that the chaotic conditions in her home centered around her, but there was a definite, remediable reason for her jumpy nerves and outbursts of temper. This woman, like so many others, was simply too busy!

Until the cause of her nerve-fatigue was removed, all her efforts to overcome, backfired. Actually, they only increased the problem.

I intend to devote an entire chapter to the problem of busyness. The point I want to make with this illustration now, is this: We must understand what the real, underlying issues are! If we batter at the gates of heaven for help, we need to know why we need help. God did not give us minds to gather cobwebs or even stardust. He gave them to us to use (See chapter 4). For now, we must get hold of the wonderful possibility that the God who created us in no way expects us to muddle through our lives, waiting for the "last day" when we can stumble through the pearly gates and collapse into eternal bliss.

God cannot be alarmed, or He would surely be when He sees His loved ones, day after day, muddling along down here, with our heads stuck into confusion-padded bags, complaining about the fact that we can't see! We don't see because we don't look. And too often, when we look, we don't look in the logical places.

Many of you will have read one or more of my other books. If you have, you know already that I do not write from a pedestal of immunity. In many areas of my life, I am still muddling along. But with great joy and certainty, I assure you, this is not God's idea for us! During the days when my head is out of my bag of confusion about myself and my real problems, I find I'm quite able to cope with whatever those days bring by way of difficult situations. During the days when, for one reason or another, I decide to stay closed inside my own stuffy viewpoint, I muddle along too.

We can all stop muddling and *look*. But this takes time. It is a growth process and God does not work superficially. He never acts in a way with us that will temporarily ease our strain. He works for eternity. He longs for us to be at home with Him forever. Comfortable in the clear light of His holy insight. "All day long, I have stretched out my hands toward a rebellious people, crying 'Behold me! Behold me!'"

So, all day long, God holds out His own insights to us, offering them with all the love of the very heart of Love. Of course, no one on this earth will ever understand all of God's ways. "My ways are higher than your ways." But always, God remains simple with us. He will give us His viewpoint and His clarity of insight according to our ability and capacity to receive.

The jittery lady who thought her prayers for a better disposition were not being heard, was merely praying amiss. She was asking for the wrong thing because she was looking in the wrong place for the cause of her problem. When she began to talk over her activity and work schedule with God, things began to happen! Like millions of other women, she was simply expecting too much of herself.

God does not expect us to be super-women. He only expects us to be *His* women, and to take the daily provision He yearns to give us.

A wife does not refuse her husband's provision for her needs, why does she refuse to take God's supply? Mainly, I think, because she is not straight about what He is trying to give her. God never gets confused. He always has everything straight. Confusion is natural to us. Therefore, one of the biggest provisions He makes for us is the gift of His own clear-minded insight into the *real causes* of our confusion. No matter how hard or how long you work, you cannot untangle a knotted up skein of yarn until you find at least one end of it.

There must be a starting place. And the starting place must be *reality*.

The young mother who finally stopped agitating in the dark about the real cause of her disposition collapse and got down to facts concerning her foolishly crowded activity schedule, said a penetrating and logical thing:

"Oh, *now* I understand!"

She did. We heap coals of *false guilt* upon our heads when we flail ourselves for simply reacting normally under the wrong conditions we have allowed to accumulate around us or within us. Her face lighted up because she was lighted up in the part of her being which God created with the ability to *understand*. The dictionary defines *understanding* as "discernment, comprehension or interpretation." In one sense this is a progressive definition. Doesn't discernment lead to comprehension (knowing), and doesn't knowing lead to interpretation of real causes?

If I can *see*, then I can *know*, and if I know, then I can *interpret* the facts. I can sort them out, eliminate, add, lessen, enlarge.

One of the first things we must understand is what is really meant by *peace*. Right now, examine your own concept of the state of mind and heart which you may think of as *peace*.

What does it really mean to you? What could make you peaceful now? What comes to your mind first? Would it be financial help? A change in your husband's viewpoint? Your children's conversion? A new house? A long vacation? A mind free from worries and problems? Perhaps that last suggestion covers everything for you.

But does it?

A baby's brain is smooth. It has no worries and no problems to solve. Would you want a baby's brain at your age? I wouldn't. An adult mind free from challenge in the form of problems and difficulties, would be an altogether dull mind. In fact, the human mind does not seem able to stay free from problems. If it sheds one batch, nine times out of ten, it will simply invent new ones.

Real peace does not mean we suddenly are transported to a problem-free realm where nothing bad ever happens. Real peace means we can survive the chaos and confusion around us without becoming chaotic or confused.

There is no such thing as an "easy peace." If you are looking for that, I suggest you close this book and buy one of the endless number available which claim to give you a kind of mental panacea. If you recite the 23rd Psalm every night before you go to sleep, and really think about it, you will be soothed temporarily. But you will only be really strengthened inwardly, you will only be given real, tough, durable inner *peace*, if you come to realize and recognize the firm grip of the hand of the One who *is* already your Shepherd!

God Himself, of course, is the answer to every human problem, but He is not a divine magician who waves problems away. He gives you *peace* that is real and eternal because in the midst of your problems He gives you Himself.

"He is our peace," wrote the high-strung, problem-laden Apostle Paul.

God is and will always be the source of all true peace. But we are not going to be so glib as to goad you into false guilt by stopping here with merely stating that truth. The purpose of this book is to attempt to help you grasp the need for *understanding* on your part. You see, it is almost as though God's hands are tied as long as we do not understand *why* we are creatures of unpeace. However, while God is intensely interested in the peaceful solutions of our problems, we must remember that peace is *not* to be the goal.

In his excellent book, *Answer to Anxiety* (Concordia), Dr. Herman Gockel wrote: "Put away from your mind, now and forever, the thought that the ultimate purpose of human life on this earth is to achieve 'peace of mind' — and that Christianity is a quick and easy road to that desired end. It is a cruel perversion of the Christian faith to palm it off as a tranquilizer sent from God, to regard it as a sort of happiness pill, or to peddle it (or to buy it) as a sort of spiritual anesthetic which will put all our inner struggles to rest. Peace of mind is *not* man's ultimate purpose on earth, nor is it the ultimate purpose of the Christian faith."

God, in other words, is not primarily concerned with making life a bed of roses for us. He is concerned with *us*. Jesus warned us that on this earth we would have trouble. He certainly had lots of it! But He also said He had "overcome the world." What did He mean by that?

I believe He meant this, at least in part: You and I are here. God recognizes that. He put us here in the first place. He knows, more clearly than any human being could ever bear to know, about the real, deep-down basic cause of all human chaos. He does not expect us to float from tragedy to tragedy or from knotty problem to knotty problem with a perpetually ethereal countenance, singing subjectively saccharin songs about the happiness of our salvation, acting (and it would be *acting!*) as though nothing very bad or jarring ever happens to a child of God.

Terrible things happen to God's children all the time. The worst thing of all happened to His only begotten Son on a criminal's cross. *Calvary happened to Jesus, but He lived through it.*

Discard at once the cultish, superficial idea that Christians must always act happy whether they feel like it or not, for fear someone might criticize their God. The Christian's God can *take* criticism. And He welcomes it, particularly when it comes as a result of one of His own, daring to live *realistically*.

One of the most difficult women with whom I ever tried to converse is a Bible teacher in her sixties, who sails in and out of the classroom at the local YW each week, trailed and adored by fifty or more worshiping females all of whom think Mrs. ———— is the "most spiritual woman on earth" because she will not allow any negative conversation in her presence.

"Now, now, my dear, I know it was hard to lose your husband. But we mustn't add to our burdens by being negative!"

And then this well-meaning, much admired, scriptural frigate smiled and smiled and smiled until my face hurt just to watch her. She is not a cultist, either. She is a pillar in a fundamentalist church.

If the agony on the face of the little widow, as she tried to smile too, hadn't been so fearful, I'm afraid I would have been graceless enough to have laughed! Don't I believe in the positive approach? With all my heart. Don't I think we should shun repeating our sad stories? Indeed I do. My point in bringing up this pathetically esteemed Bible lady? Just this: I found it almost impossible to talk with her because she was totally *unrealistic*. She never touched the earth which binds us all if we are honest.

The little widow needed a sister in Christ to weep with her first. After all, her husband had only died the month before.

It is simply not realistic to expect to *feel* peaceful when your heart is torn by grief. It is near madness to think you are slipping spiritually (or that someone else will think you are!) if you do not *feel* peaceful when your child is dangerously ill. If your husband has just lost his job. If you have just lost yours.

Let's keep this straight. We will not be speaking of living through your problems so that you can always, every day, in every way, *feel* more and more peaceful. We will be speaking of *how* we can strip off the trappings from around our minds and hearts, so that the One who *is* peace, Himself, can get at us to heal us.

We will, for the next eight chapters, take eight basic problems and attempt to *understand* how together or separately, they can be the *real sources* of our human dilemma. (I have chosen these eight problems because they seem to be the main genuine causes of confusion among the women with whom I talk and correspond. They are not chosen from the books of any "scholarly authority." They come from you who read my books.) After we have discussed these eight problems in Chapters 2 through 9, we will then try to relate them to human relationships; to show how they can be the *real causes* of our problems within the family and among our friends and neighbors.

We will not be speaking about a technique for living through your present problems toward a non-existent Utopia where no more problems will plague you ever, ever again. We will be speaking about the fact that we all have and we will always have problems. But these problems need not leave us in a shambles emotionally! We *can* live through them. We can do more than muddle through, we can *live* through. And daily, in little, hidden ways and big outward ways, we can become more and more at home with the One who Himself longs to *be* our peace.

2: The Problem of Doubt

2:

THE PROBLEM OF DOUBT

Take a long, objective look at yourself. Are you a "stop and start" Christian? Do you have to start all over again every time something goes wrong in your life? Are you only occasionally sure of this *peace* Jesus said He would leave with us? Are you unable to live through your problems from confusion to peace and adequacy?

Do you run to your pastor or your best friend (or the one who is the most long-suffering with you) and go through the whole agonizing bit all over again every time something disturbing happens? Are you always reaching for God? Trying (all over again) to "get through to Him" every time you hit a bump? Is there some patient soul who gets a phone call from you every time you bang your knees on a problem? Do you jerk the hooks of friendship in the heart of your friend by presenting your troubled self by telephone or in person as though to say: "Well, here I am in a mess again — what are you going to do about me this time?"

What you are really saying is: "Well, here I am in a mess again — what are you and your all-powerful God going to do about me?"

We need each other for burden sharing, but if you keep a path beaten to someone's door delivering *your* problems with sickening regularity, you are not only imposing on that friend, you are doubting God.

Perhaps it would be well to say this now: If you are plagued night and day with doubts, you may need professional help. If it only seems to upset you more when some calm Christian reassures you concerning the fidelity of God, then you probably do need psychological help in learning *how* to control your own thoughts. It is no disgrace to consult a professional counselor or psychologist or psychiatrist. No more than it is a disgrace to consult a medical doctor when a virus attacks your breathing apparatus. If you are harrassed by doubts in general, including God and people, then you need outside help. (If possible, for your own sake *and* mine, try to find help nearby. I do the best I can, but I am *not* a professional counselor and I do not have a regular secretary and I cannot give you adequate help, nor can anyone else, by letter. I am giving you the very best I have to offer in my books.) If you are a chronic doubter, and if these doubts have reached alarming proportions so that your personality is distorted because of them, make an appointment at once with a competent counselor or psychiatrist. It may be that old patterns need breaking up. This takes time and skill on the part of the doctor and cooperation from you. Most likely your minister, if he has become aware of the importance of the human mind in action in the life of faith, will be able to tell you in one visit whether or not you need medical treatment.

If you have a reasonably normal mind like most women, but are still a "stop and start" Christian, full of chaos and uncertainty about relationship with God, take some time out right now to think clearly about yourself in the presence of the One who is always thinking clearly about you. He can help and help permanently.

In my book, *Woman to Woman,* there is a chapter on the difference it makes in a woman's *spiritual life* if Christ is in control of her personality. I wrote that chapter from a heart bursting with immediate concern for my then current group of correspondents who were "nervous wrecks" concerning the state of their relationships with God. I hope you have either read that chapter, or will read it — if possible before you read this one.

Since the publication of *Woman to Woman,* I have had many letters which showed plainly that these women had settled down to walk with Christ, minus their previous emotional agitation, after having read that chapter. But I have had others too. In fact, it is rare when a week passes by without one or more letters from women who have read *Woman to Woman,* but who are still full of doubts and turmoil about God. These letters discouraged me at first, but I took them all to Jesus Christ and talked them over with Him. We talked about each woman who wrote, but we also talked about what else might be needed to help them.

In the chapter concerning our *spiritual life* in *Woman to Woman,* I emphasized God's part. Realizing that His heart is always in motion toward us is the stabilizing thing to me. However, when I discussed the matter with Him before writing this book, I seemed to be convinced that for a certain type of woman, emphasis must also be given to *her* part.

I said something like this to Him: "Lord, You know that many women go along through happy days and troubled days *without* continuing or even spasmodic periods of really destructive doubt. Why? You know also that *Your* intentions toward the doubting women are as generous as they are toward those who do not doubt. You do not love those who refuse doubts one bit more than you love the doubters. So why are they plagued with doubts about their relationship with You? What is the difference between those who do not consider 'giving up' in the Christian life and those who seem always to be about to 'give up'?"

Two things came to me. First, I remembered Thomas, Jesus' disciple. A lot of things about Thomas cleared up for me also, as I wrote *Beloved World.* One of them is the fact that we are wrong to use a disparaging tone of voice when we call a person a "doubting Thomas." This man's doubts were healthy. Perhaps yours are, too. Thomas was a man who simply could not live with an unasked question. He had to have an answer his inquiring mind could accept. He was a pessimist by nature, and pessimists need convincing. To have healthy doubts is not wrong. In fact, it can lead to complete conviction. In some cases, a conviction stronger than that of a person who believes at once everything he's told.

Jesus understood Thomas' mind. He understands yours. God really knows us, exactly as we are. (See my book, *Strictly Personal.*) We are no mystery to Him, and just as Jesus was with Thomas, so He will still be with us. You remember that when the risen Master appeared to His frightened, heart-broken men locked in a darkened room after His crucifixion, Thomas was not there. His kind of doubting, pessimistic mind often prefers to grieve alone. All the men were grief-stricken. Their glorious highway had suddenly become a shadowy dead-end road! Their Master was dead. The others locked themselves in a room together. Thomas went away somewhere by himself. This is neither right nor wrong. It was simply Thomas's personality. But Jesus knew this. And so He came back the next week — just for Thomas. After awhile, Thomas had joined the others, still afraid to believe Jesus was alive, in spite of their jubilation. Jesus knew the very noise of their jubilation and joy would only upset thoughtful Thomas more than ever. The Master knew His doubting disciple still would not be able to believe. So He did for Thomas what He will do for anyone today — He made a special trip back, and then Thomas believed utterly! (Read John 20:19-30.)

So doubts, if we are open to having them disappear, as Thomas was, are not always bad. We need to be honest here, however. Some women (and men) cling to their doubts knowingly or unknowingly. Usually they are not aware of it, but doubts can be real attention-getters and strong alibis for disobedience!

We will have more to say about "attention getting" in a moment, but check now on your obedience. Are you "doubting" because if you suddenly stopped, you would have to obey God on some point which is uncomfortable for you?

The second thing God gave me when I went to Him for help in writing this chapter had to do with the caliber and *length* of our commitment to Him. He seemed to be saying to me: "My daughter, some of My children simply never consider 'giving up.' They stumble, they rebel, they grieve, they are perplexed, they fail, they are hurt, but it never seems to occur to them to rule Me out. Even when they don't understand Me, their hearts are *committed hearts*. Even when they disobey, I can see that I am still included in their plans. They committed their lives to Me and that settles it. They suffer and sometimes they grow confused about their own problems, but they never grow confused about the fact that I am *in* the problem with them! This is not necessarily a virtue, it is simply the state of their minds toward Me. Their minds are 'fixed' once and for all. Not on their problems, but on Me."

Great light can break through your winter sky right here!

What does commitment mean to you? Maybe I should have asked "how many times have you 'totally' committed yourself to God?" I hope you are smiling. If you are, you are beginning to see a *real issue* come into focus. Oh, I know commitments can be broken, and in that case we need re-commitment. But think now, could it be that many of your "spiritual upheavals" are due to the fact that although *emotionally* or *sentimentally* you committed your life to Christ, you neglected to settle it with your *will?*

When a woman marries a man, she marries him "for better or for worse." If the bride and groom are both Christian, the agreement is for the duration of life on this earth — "until death do us part." There is nothing in the marriage ceremony which says that a woman commits herself to a man only for "better." It says "for better or for worse." In other words, for all time, through all things, under all circumstances, this woman will remain in the marriage *relationship* with this man. Could it be that there is so much "giving up" when the marital waters get rough (as I understand they usually do), because one or both members of the wedding did not really commit themselves once and for all?

God has further verified His word to me on this matter of commitment by way of my dear friend, Dr. Anna B. Mow, through whom He can always speak to me directly. Her friendship and counsel are among my choicest gifts from God. (And if you would like to share some of the real help I've received in her friendship, I've done you a favor you didn't know about. I kept talking until Anna Mow wrote her own book — *Say Yes to Life!* Zondervan). If you have not read it, by all means waste no more time.

Anna Mow and I were having one of our rare, relaxed days in which we could just talk and be together in a motel room in Indiana sometime ago, during a speaking engagement of hers. We sat in comfortable chairs, in a comfortable lack of clothes, with our feet up on opposite sides of my bed. We are both well past forty, and neither of us was her most glamorous that particular "day off!" I stress this point, because it is relevant to my story. Anna was glancing at the morning paper. Marilyn Monroe had just been married again, and Anna read the story aloud with great tenderness and pity that the girl had such trouble finding happiness in her various tries at matrimony. After she finished reading, she looked at me and declared: "Now, Genie, the difference between Marilyn Monroe and *me* is this — I'm *committed* to Baxter!"

Baxter is her husband. They are grandparents now (twelve times I think) and I am sure, with two strong personalities such as theirs, the "sea of matrimony" has rocked their disposition-boat many times. But Anna and Baxter would never have considered giving up! They had committed themselves to each other and that was that. Of course, they had problems to work through during their long life of missionary service in India. They still have them, I'm sure, in their years of "retirement." Who doesn't have problems? The point of this book is that problems can be lived *through* — all the way through and out the other side! When two people live through their problems together, they only strengthen their ties with each other.

When we live through our problems *with God,* we come out the other side of the problem more convinced than ever that He *is* the way.

What is the state of *your commitment* to God?

Is it chopped up by prolonged doubts and stops and starts? Like the much-divorced women of this world, are you committed to Him only as long as things are going pretty well? If so, then you are like my alcoholic friend, who thinks she has to make a big, dramatic scene of surrender — plead for God's attention, take my time and her energy to "find" God all over again every time she falls off the wagon. God is never lost! The act of receiving forgiveness from God does not have to be cloaked in dramatics. In fact, the gift of forgiveness is so great in its cost to God, it stuns me to silence.

In my opinion, my alcoholic friend "commits" herself to God only from one binge to another. But I don't preach, because only she and the Holy Spirit will know when it is the real thing on her part.

It is always the real thing with God.

We tend to preach and plead and try to persuade people to commit their lives to Christ. This is holy ground on which we tread, and we dare not stamp around on it insensitively in our zeal for numbers we can boast about! People cannot be persuaded by other people to commit their lives. The person with the life in hand must do this — alone with God.

Perhaps you have just never seriously considered the duration of your own commitment to Him. When He received you, He did not guarantee happiness in the process. Jesus did warn us that in this world there would be plenty of trouble. For everyone — Christians and non-Christians alike. If your relationship with God goes on the rocks periodically, perhaps it is because your "commitment" is only for the duration of your own *conscious* inner peace. Re-read our first chapter. The *peace of God* is the kind of peace which can take whatever life hands it.

A woman in her fifties wrote recently: "I became a

Christian five years ago and they were five of the happiest years of my life. Then my son and husband died and since then I have never been able to feel like anything real happened to me with God!"

Her tragedy was two-fold. A heart-breaking thing for any woman to take. But wasn't her commitment with God limited by the events of her life? When I pointed this out to her, she was able and willing to see. This woman did not want to go on being a burden to her friends and pastor. She wanted to face the real issue. When she did, she realized nothing at all had happened to her relationship with God through all her grief. Our God is an everlasting God. His commitment to us is from the beginning and it is forever.

I find myself unable to be kind to my doubts because I despise anything that rocks my commitment to the God who has always been fully committed to me!

Some commitments to Christ are limited by the person's childish demand for attention from other human beings. This is a familiar story to ministers and Christian counselors. As long as some selected human being is paying "enough attention" to the person with overwhelming problems, well and good. He or she will go on "growing in the faith." Especially if his or her counselor is constantly bragging up the spiritual growth of the problem child. But let the counselor become busy with someone else's problems (or, heaven forbid, her own) and bang! The problem child consciously or unconsciously finds a way to create another crisis between herself and God.

Is your commitment to the God of Calvary conditioned by the amount of attention you are getting from your spiritual advisor? You always have God's *full attention*. Isn't that enough?

I believe also that many persons, perhaps quite unconsciously, create spiritual crises just to relieve their own boredom. This is never true, if the caliber of our commitment has been such that God has been able to give us some of His own concern for other people. We will be too busy to be bored.

The seeds of doubt fly on the winds stirred up by every human crisis. They drop with regularity into everyone's mind. But they can only take root and grow into troublesome "baobab" trees if we encourage them! I despise my doubts and refuse them ground, because they threaten to throw me back once more into that state of confusion through which I trudged as a non-believer. I'm sick of confusion. I'm finished with chaos. Peace has spoiled me. God has not "spoiled" me as a mother can spoil her child, but He has lived with me through my problems, giving me grace and insight and enough inner balance to be able to cope with my life. I have decided this central issue of commitment once and for all. A "committed Christian" is not necessarily a spiritual giant. It is simply someone who has made up his or her mind to follow Christ. Commitment requires no masterful stroke of super-spirituality on my part. It is simply deciding which life I want — the life of confusion or the life of peace and adequacy. There will be problems in both.

God is always pressing toward us with love, but He needs the open path of our basic commitment in order to care for us as He longs to do. *We* decide whether or not we will clear the path or keep it cluttered with doubts.

3: The Problem of Ingratitude

3:

THE PROBLEM OF INGRATITUDE

One heart-breaking incident comes to my mind invariably when I think on the *problem of ingratitude*.

Several years ago, I was being entertained in the home of the lady who had handled the scheduling of my speaking engagement in her church. She was a deeply disturbed woman. I sensed this from the moment she and her husband picked me up at the local airport. When I had been in her home a few hours, I knew at least part of the reason for her highly nervous state — her relationship with her husband.

They both tried to make things pleasant for me, and they did extend me every courtesy, but their attractive ranch home fairly crackled with discontent and friction. The three small children were out of control most of the time.

I had been in my room studying less than an hour when I heard someone come in the front door. It was another woman. I ignored the somewhat agitated conversation until it could no longer be ignored.

"Eugenia Price is a guest in my house and I won't have you making trouble while she's here!" my hostess snapped, forgetting to stage whisper.

The angry talk broke off abruptly and I could hear a woman's quick footsteps pass my door. Another door opened down the hall, slammed shut, and there was silence in the house, except for my hostess bustling noisily around her kitchen preparing dinner alone. The other woman, whoever it was, did not help her.

Needless to say, I felt uneasy. I was not scheduled to speak until the next morning, and I determined right then to spend the entire evening in my room — if possible.

Dinner was an excruciating ordeal. Fortunately, they had sent the children to a neighbor's house to eat. It was quieter that way, but the conversational barbs flew from wife to husband, from mother-in-law to son-in-law, from husband to wife, from mother to daughter and from daughter to mother. Yes, the woman I had heard arguing with my hostess before dinner was her mother, who had come for an extended visit.

They "honored" me with worked-on smiles as the barbs continued to fly, as though to say, "We are only kidding!" But they weren't kidding.

After dinner, I went to the kitchen and offered to help my hostess with the dishes. She was as embittered as the other two, but somehow she touched me. Of course, she refused my offer flatly.

"I wouldn't think of letting you help! Anyway, this is what I'm for — dishwashing."

I just stood there and smiled at her a moment.

"Well — that's right. I'm not good for another thing around this place!" Then she tried a smile. "Please go in the living room and talk with Mother and my husband."

"I came out here because I'd rather be with you, if you don't mind," I said, meaning it.

She looked about ready to burst into tears. "Really?"

"Yes, really."

She handed me a clean dishtowel from the drawer beneath her kitchen sink and we began doing dishes.

Instinctively I kept my voice down. "Does your mother visit you regularly?"

She looked at me almost relieved. "Too regularly. Once a year. But this is an extra one. My husband is going away on business tomorrow and she came to help with the children!" She forced a laugh and then stopped washing the glasses and leaned against her sink and whispered, "I hope you can forgive us all. We were terribly rude at dinner. We're always this way. It's bad enough when Mother isn't here. When she's here, everything gets worse! I love my mother — I guess, but I'm so sick and tired hearing that I should have married someone else, that I don't handle my children well, that we shouldn't be stuck here in this small town away from the 'opportunities' of life and so on and on and on — I'm so sick and tired of hearing how she sacrifices her precious time to come here to this hick town to help me, when none of us wants her! Oh, I'd like to be glad to see her when she comes. But how can I be? My husband and I have enough trouble with our own lives without her coming to help us along to more trouble!"

"Oh-h-h!"

We both turned, startled by the shriek of anger. There in the doorway stood Mother!

"So *that's* the gratitude I get for making that hard trip all the way from Los Angeles to this dreadful little berg! Now, Miss Price, you've heard it for yourself. Not once, not once, mind you, in all the years I've been coming, has anyone in this house made me feel at home. Not even wanted, mind you. Not even wanted in the house of my only daughter!"

Her voice rose higher and higher. My hostess turned her back and began to sob. The mother was shouting now, almost out of control. I hadn't seen the beginning of a tantrum like that since I used to watch my childhood play-mate "throw her fits" every time the doctor came to examine her.

"I'm just not wanted nor appreciated anywhere! Is this the kind of thanks a mother gets for sacrificing all her life so her daughter can have everything? I'm not good for anything but a buffer between these two, Miss Price!"

Tears streamed down the mother's angry, reddened face now, as she turned her tirade on me.

"I'm good for nothing but a buffer between these two people. It's bad enough that they fight all the time before their children when I'm not here, but wouldn't you think they'd act civilized when I come? I don't understand it. I just don't understand it!"

The older woman ran screeching in self-pity out of the kitchen and down the basement steps. Her hysterical sobs went on long after the front door slammed behind the helpless husband. He didn't know anything to do but get out. I wanted to, but I didn't have anywhere to go.

I had already planned to speak the next morning on *gratitude*. The mother wasn't there, of course. She had made herself ill. My hostess, I'm glad to say, began to *understand*. Even at her age, after all the years of being her unfortunate self, the mother could have understood, if she had been open. She, like the daughter, like you and me, could understand *if* she wanted to, that self-pity, lostness, inferiority feelings, bitterness, even indifference are direct results of basic *ingratitude*.

If she could have been *grateful* that she was able to be a "buffer" between these two, her whole outlook would have changed.

Ingratitude snaps shut the human heart. Grateful hearts are always open hearts. They are hearts which have received. Even God cannot squeeze a blessing through a closed heart. The Apostle Paul tells us we are to give thanks always for all things to God. Is this possible? Is it possible for us to give thanks for a newly broken heart? For the death of a loved one? For the opportunity of being a "buffer"?

If we have *cultivated* the attitude of giving thanks, yes.

If we have gone along giving lip-service gratitude before our more than adequate meals, and little more, no. If we have merely sung "Praise God from whom all blessings flow" in church on Sunday morning, and have never spent even five minutes in private praise to Him for Himself, no. If we have written checks to missions because it is the thing to do (and because it is deductible) and have never given ourselves to a needy person out of sheer gratitude to God for the gift of Himself, no. It is totally unrealistic for us to expect to be able suddenly to reap the benefit of grateful hearts.

When Paul landed in Rome in chains, an old man,

buffeted on every side, we are told that he "gave thanks and took courage." Obviously, his act of giving thanks (of being truly grateful) opened the path for God to pour down the needed courage. But if Paul had not been in the habit of giving thanks, if the natural state of his heart had not been *gratitude,* he could not, at that difficult time, have been truly grateful, no matter how hard he might have tried.

We need to form the habit of *gratitude.* It can change everything! It never occurred to me to thank God for the ample supply of hot water in my house until the tank went out of commission one day. Now my daily shower is even more refreshing because I have formed the *habit* of gratitude for the hot water. I don't always put it into words — "God, thank You for this good hot water." But I remember to be grateful. The water itself reminds me.

This would not be so, however, if I did not have any interest in *awareness.* How aware are you? Do you take your shower with your mind on a dozen other things? Do you prepare your children's breakfast with your mind busy well into the afternoon's women's meeting? I fail to see how we can even begin to establish the habit of gratitude if we fail to keep ourselves aware of the moment and its small goodnesses.

How long has it been since you have looked at your husband and felt really aware of him? Aware that he is yours? That he loves you. That you are in this thing together. Most likely, if your marriage is even ordinarily successful, a few moments of such awareness will lead your heart quite naturally to thanking God for this man.

The pathetic mother in the story with which we opened this chapter was literally bursting with *self-pity.* What would one tiny streak of gratitude have done for that woman? For the daughter and her husband for that matter. They were all three sorry for themselves. They all three felt *inferior.* No one felt really needed. The mother made more noise about it, but they were all three riddled with feelings of inferiority. One little start toward being grateful to God for health, for food, for His love, begins at once to make us feel less *inferior*. If He cares enough to give us these things — maybe we have been exaggerating our pitiable plight! An ungrateful heart is a blind heart. It cannot see its blessings until it begins to give thanks.

In my opinion, the most glorious singing voice I have ever heard was the almost unbelievably beautiful contralto voice of Kathleen Ferrier. Miss Ferrier died of cancer when she was still a young woman. From her hospital bed she wrote to a close friend: "Well, here I sit in bed counting my blessings!"

Can the debilitating feeling of *lostness* be overcome by thanksgiving? Indeed it can be. I have watched my own mother prove this in the past year. After my father's death, she sold her lovely home where we had all been so happy together and bought what she honestly believed to be good income property. It was zoned for apartments, and the price she got for her house was just enough to buy the income property and remodel it. She was elated and even told me long distance, that I didn't have to worry about her on moving day, because she was so excited about the new prospects, she wouldn't be too sorry to leave our lovely home on the hill. Then the avalanche struck! Even though the property she was buying was zoned for apartments, the building inspector refused for political reasons to permit her to do the necessary remodeling.

Mother was beside herself. The house on the hill was already sold. The money, all we had left after my father's long illness, had changed hands. She had already bought the so-called "income property." Moving day was a nightmare of *lostness* for her! *Self-pity*, a luxury Mother seldom permits herself, took over. Unlike the woman in our first story, who was caught in a trap of habitual self-pity and ingratitude, Mother had plenty of facts to back up her plight. She was stuck with a huge old house, which would cost a small fortune to heat, her money was tied up in it and the only income she could salvage was from the rental of 4 of the 12 rooms! Without building an elaborate outside concrete stairway, she would not even be allowed to rent the third floor. Of course, she was sorry for herself. Of course, she felt lost. She even felt unnecessary but understandable guilt for having bought the house at all!

She is still in the same predicament and a year has passed. Her income from renting her four rooms does not operate the large house. It is difficult to sell. Who would want to get into the same spot? And yet, this past Christmas, I watched my mother fill our "new" home with light and *praise* to the One whose birthday she and I really celebrated. She greeted me one morning with: "Darling, let's light every lamp and every candle in the house. He came to earth! We have a reason to celebrate!"

Her problem is not solved — far from it. What happened to her anxiety and her self-pity and her feeling of lostness? For awhile, it was like losing my father all over again, and although she tried to spare me, I was dragged down under her heavy load, too.

What happened? *She remembered to be grateful.* She had to start slowly. But she started. Hers is a heart brimming with thanksgiving these days. And with it, her natural *indifference* toward the problems of other people has turned into the kind of Christlike caring that is a real challenge to her daughter! Nothing is settled where her problem is concerned, but *she* is settled.

My mother had human reason to be *bitter* too. As bitter as the mother in our first story surely was. An edge of bitterness crept in now and then. But as the *gratitude* grew, the *bitterness* vanished. This seems to be a spiritual law. A dependable one. But no law is of any value unless we try it.

With all my heart, I believe that poor hysterical woman, who went screaming down the basement stairs of her daughter's home, could find her way out, if she could only find a way to open her heart in gratitude—even for one small thing.

Ingratitude had warped her entire personality. Of course, she felt lost and unwanted and inferior and indifferent to the hearts of other people. Of course, she was sorry for herself. She was in a pitiable condition, and she was hugging her pitiable condition with all her might.

How grateful is your heart right now as you read this page? On the very night before they crucified Him, Jesus "took the cup and gave thanks." Things were not going well for Him that night! But He gave thanks anyway.

Gratitude was the normal state of His heart.

If your life is good, if things are going well for you, if your cup is running over, don't stop with a fleeting period of guilt for not having been thankful enough. No point in wasting time with that. Simply begin to give thanks. Give thanks if your cup is filled with sweetness and drink it with grace. Give thanks also, if your cup is only half-full or even filled with trouble, and drink it with grace. Grace is available for us all under all conditions. Grace to give thanks to our Father. The grace Jesus Christ brings into the human life is never limited by the circumstances of that life.

The heart that is truly open to God is a thankful heart in good times and in bad. The "times" do not influence it one way or another. Here, in a *continuing* state of inner gratitude, lies one of the big keys to the stable human life.

Gratitude may not change the conditions surrounding your problem. It has not changed my mother's problem at all, but it has changed her. She is now *living through* her problem, with inner quiet, poise and adequacy.

This is authentic Christianity in action for the world to see. And oh how the world needs to see!

4: The Problem of Ignorance

4:

THE PROBLEM OF IGNORANCE

Perhaps you are surprised at my use of the word *ignorance* as a source of human problems. According to the dictionary, one can be ignorant, *i. e.* "without knowledge in general, or in a particular matter." We will concern ourselves with the "particular matters" in which far too many of us *are* ignorant.

I want to differentiate now, between the content of this chapter and the next, which will deal with the problem areas resulting from *darkness*. There, we will be speaking of *darkness*, not from ignorance, but as opposed to the light revealed by God through His Holy Spirit. The Christian woman has access to two kinds of knowledge: That which she acquires through her own efforts and concentration, and that given by God as revealed knowledge. Both are His gifts.

As far as I can see, God would like to have us all make the maximum use of the brain He has given us. He does not expect us to sit and wait for heavenly lightning to strike. He expects us to make use of both means of acquiring knowledge — through our own intellectual efforts as well as by His direct revelation.

There was never a human mind so keen, so controlled, so adequate to every problem, so truly exercised and learned, as the mind of Jesus of Nazareth. We are instructed in God's

Word to "let that mind be in you, which was in Christ Jesus!"

Can we be as authoritative and as mentally alert as He was? In one sense, yes. His mind was not streaked with sin, and in that respect we could never have His mind. But we can have His *attitude* of mind and without doubt, that was an attitude of total alertness and energy. Jesus of Nazareth *used* His mind constantly. So can we. We can attain to the caliber of the mind of Christ, in spite of the fact that we are still in the process of pressing "toward the goal of the high calling in Christ Jesus."

To have the mind that was in Christ Jesus should be our goal, but pressing toward that goal should not mean an increased burden for us. If we are realistic in our thinking, we will see the development of our minds as a stimulating adventure. I find myself beginning to hate the waste of my mental laziness. God is not adding a burden when He tells us through Paul that we should have the mind of Christ. He never adds to our burdens. If He does, then Jesus was wrong, because He said, "My yoke is easy and My burden is light." When we are instructed to have the "mind which was in Christ Jesus" this does not mean that we are to begin cringing in shame and false guilt because we are not mental giants like the Man from Nazareth. It means that we are to become gratefully interested in doing what He did — develop to their maximum the minds we already have.

Some of us are slow witted, others are quick. The truth is, I feel sure, that no woman ever developed her mind fully. No man, for that matter, except Jesus.

It is essential right here, for us to think realistically about human minds. They are not all the same. In one family, there can be one brilliant child and two or three who are average. Certainly, the brilliant child should never be held up as an example for the others. This is not being realistic. Persons with average or limited mentalities simply cannot think in the same way as those with superior mental equipment. We all know this, but we seldom act as though we know it. We despise or look down on slow minds. This is as ridiculous as despising a weak body because it cannot jump high hurdles. What we need to begin to despise is the laziness that keeps a mind slow or a body weak. If we were more realistic about the natural equipment of the people we know, fifty per cent of our tendency to judge would drop away! Our judgments would become accurate and tolerant and helpful. They would stop stinging and tearing down. They would begin to build.

The truth remains, however, that we can all, regardless of the caliber of our inherited mental equipment, make the most of what we have been given.

Of course, we need to be selective in acquiring knowledge. But being intelligently *selective* is a different thing from being *narrow* in the areas of knowledge to which we expose our minds.

Lack of *exposure* is the big problem where ignorance is concerned. How do you know you do not like Brahms' First Symphony, for example, if you have never exposed yourself to it? I am not suggesting forcing yourself, merely *exposing* your open mind and senses.

When my brother Joe and I were young, Mother bought three season tickets to the local civic music concerts. We were both equally exposed to classical music. I loved it, my brother fidgeted and complained that his trousers were too tight. Mother did not force him to go. She explained that she was only trying to find out what we each liked and in no way made him feel inferior to his sister. He was not. He was just *different*. (He has an adept mechanical turn of mind. I can't even drive a car without an automatic gear shift! She was not trying to make an artist of Joe or an engineer of me. She was merely exposing our minds.)

How do you know that you can't understand politics if you have not spent some time during the year preceding the election studying the voting records of congressmen and the outcome of peace talks?

How do you know you can't make "head or tail" of all this outer space question if you have never exposed yourself to some of the simply written articles on the subject?

How do you know you don't like modern art if you have never read or listened to some of the creative ideas in the minds of the men and women who are painting today?

For that matter, persons who insist they are not interested in God, can't really know this to be true, until they have *exposed* their minds to His mind — their hearts to His heart. A man needs to discover God for himself. He is waving his flag of ignorance when he rejects the claims of Jesus Christ without ever having spent any time learning about the One whom he is rejecting.

There is a glaring contradiction in the reasoning of a person who scoffs at something he or she knows nothing about. This is true for non-Christians, but it is also true for Christians. The Christian woman has the reputation of God to consider when she presents her personality to the world. People who do not know our God judge Him by us. We are just as contradictory as they, when we present lopsided intelligences versed only in religious matters.

A Christian woman should be as clear as possible in her own thinking about God. I don't know what I would have done without Christian literature. I need the ideas of other Christians to supplement and clarify my own. I need them for comparison and for help in understanding my Bible. I do not agree with every author's opinion, but this only stimulates my own thinking. I have never been afraid to *think* daringly about God. After all, if He *is* God, isn't He big enough to withstand my thoughts?

The Bible urges us repeatedly to discover what God is like! If I refuse to shed my ignorance about the God I worship, I can only expect to fall into the ancient trap of religious ignorance — *superstition.* In "enlightened" America, we have no cause to scoff at the superstition of the rest of the world, if we, ourselves, do not bend every effort to find out more and more about life *and* the Lord we follow.

I had dinner several years ago with the president of a missionary society, who had punctuated the afternoon's report on superstition in India with a regular series of "Tsk, tsk, tsks." But at dinner, she talked steadily about how God was "punishing" her evangelist son-in-law with a retarded child because the fellow had committed a moral sin in his teens!

Her ignorance appalled me much more than the report on the superstitions of India.

Either this woman had never taken time to read her Bible, or she had read it only to console herself, not bothering to *think* through the real issues involved in God's forgiveness. She was sure of her salvation and I was sure of it, too, but I was also sure she did not know much about the nature of the God who had saved her. *Forgiveness* is one of His strongest characteristics. Did she think God spoke through Jeremiah only to her, when He declared: "I will forgive their iniquity, and I will remember their sin no more"? Didn't the Word of God include her evangelist son-in-law when David wrote: "He does not deal with us according to our sins, nor requite us according to our iniquities"?

Was God apt to "requite" (get even) with her son-in-law and allow her and all the other "moral" ladies to go scot free?

This well-intentioned woman was *ignorant* about God and we can do Him no greater injustice! No thinking person could possibly be so superstitious about His conduct if he or she had taken time to find out the facts, to sort them and interpret them with average God-given intelligence.

I recently received a letter from an outstanding Christian business man, with a question asked so often it makes one wonder: "I have lived for Christ for fifteen years now. I have honestly tried to be Christian in my business relationships. For some reason, however, I am losing money steadily. Is God punishing me because twenty-one years ago, when I was merely a paid-up church member and did not know Christ personally, I pulled some pretty slick tricks in my business?"

"As far as the east is from the west, so far does He remove our transgressions from us." David wrote this in his psalm for this man too, and it is printed clearly in his Bible

as Psalm 103, just as it is in mine. This was an intelligent
man. His problem? He was not thinking!

Civilization has always been shackled with superstition,
due to lack of knowledge. It is quite normal that we should
drag around some of these chains today. But it is not necessary that we continue. We can learn the facts! We can
know God. "Try the spirits to see if they are of God," John
wrote. How can we do this if we are so little acquainted
with the real nature of the Spirit of God? It is *ignorance*
of the character of God which causes us to go blithely along
crediting or discrediting Him with every unexplainable thing
that happens. We are not automatons and we do not have
to do with a quixotic God. He works always according to
the sanity of His own nature! Did Jesus Christ really come
to reveal the Father's heart to us? If so, then can you imagine that fifteen years later He would have refused to heal
the child of the woman taken in adultery? Would He have
"requited" her — held it against her and gotten even with
her through the child, because she had committed an already
forgiven sin?

We need to think.

We need to think and weigh the facts made plain to us
in God's Word. Much of the dilemma of human suffering
would be cleared away if men and women were not so
ignorant of God's nature.

Superstition is a real result of *ignorance*.

False guilt is a real result of *ignorance*.

Much of both can be lived through and eliminated, as
soon as we are willing to spend some time shedding our
ignorance about the mind of God.

Fear can also be the result of *ignorance*.

Here is an excerpt from a letter which is far more
typical than you might believe. "I am a Christian and have
been for twenty-one years. But no matter how hard I pray,
for all those years I have been afraid! People have gotten
so they don't want to talk to me anymore. They always
know I'll start talking about my fears. It is getting worse
now. I am almost afraid to go outside alone."

Right here, let me say that this woman's problem had gone on so long without help, I advised her to seek professional assistance at once. There is no shame involved in getting medical help for either the body or the mind. This woman needed medical help. This does not rule out God's healing power. We insult Him when we contend that He must heal us *only* by what we call "miracle." He must prefer to work through human channels. He left His kingdom in the hands of mere human beings.

But most likely, if this pathetic woman had been informed about the viewpoint of God toward fear early in her Christian life, her situation would not have reached such an advanced state. From the rest of her letter, I judge that she had been convinced doctrinally at an early age that she would go to heaven because Jesus Christ died on His Cross for her. This much is true. But evidently she stopped *learning* there.

What is God's attitude toward human fear? He understands it! He is keenly aware of it every second that passes. He not only knows about it, He alone knows the damage it can do to His loved ones. The only answer to human fear of any kind ultimately, so far as I can see, is more *knowledge* of God Himself. The child stops being afraid at night when mother comes into the room. Why? Because of what the child knows about mother.

Once more, basically, we are confronted with *ignorance*.

Ignorance which is present because of *ignorance* of ignorance itself!

This woman just didn't think about inquiring until her fear had made her ill and was wrecking the lives of her husband and her five children.

Plainly, clearly, simply, the Bible tells us we are to "grow in the *knowledge* of the Lord Jesus Christ." Jesus Himself said, ". . . *learn* of Me, (then you will find out that) My yoke is easy and My burden is light."

My book, *Strictly Personal*, was written because I believe with all my heart, that most of the human dilemma could be lessened if people would take time to find out

about God. To learn of Him in His written down Word, the
Bible. To learn of Him as He invades the minds of those
who write Christian literature. To learn of Him in relation
to science, political thought, poetry, art and music.

Our God is not limited by *religion*.

The glorious order of His mind can be found in the
precision of an algebraic equation and the pattern of a
snowflake. His voice sings carols with the children at Christmas and whispers in an open fire on a winter afternoon.

Jesus, the Son of God, was not limited by religion. He
never used the word. He spoke of *life*. He came to bring
life. A quality of life He called *eternal*. To learn of Him is
to learn of life. "I am . . . the life," He said.

"Without Him was not anything made that was made."

He created our minds and He has every right to expect
us to use them.

When we think through to the real issues, weighing
them in the light of God's revealed word to us — when we
shed *ignorance* on any creative subject, we obey God.

When we obey God, we begin to find our way *through*
our problems. He does not ask obedience in order to satisfy
a whim of His. He asks obedience for our sakes. No one
hates any problem that limits the human heart as intensely
as God hates it.

And He hates our *ignorance* because He loves us so
much!

5: The Problem of Darkness

5:

THE PROBLEM OF DARKNESS

Let me begin by making it clear that in urging women to use their God-given minds in order to cope with the problems which result from *ignorance*, I did *not* state that knowledge of God could be obtained through the mind alone.

In Chapter 4, on *ignorance*, we thought solely from the standpoint of *our part* in the necessary cooperation with God. We, and we alone, are responsible for the extent of our own ignorance. Granted, everyone cannot be university trained, but everyone can study and everyone can learn.

Everyone can expose herself or himself to new ideas. Everyone can stretch the horizons of his or her mind. This is not up to God. This is up to us. And we can't do it unless we are willing to make the necessary schedule rearrangements and take the necessary steps, however inconvenient. Instead of the word *ignorant*, we could have used the word *laziness*, but not quite so inclusively. With ignorance, we include us all! Everyone is not lazy. But we all do have areas of unknowing about which we can do something.

As we all have areas of *ignorance*, so we all have areas of *darkness*. Perhaps it would be well here to make some differentiation between spiritual *darkness* and spiritual *blindness*. The difference is subtle, so think carefully.

As I understand it, darkness implies no light present.

Blindness can mean light is present, but the person just does not see.

Either he *does* not see or he *cannot* see or he *will* not see. Why not stop reading a moment and think of the persons you know (yourself included) who seem spiritually blind on certain points? Are they looking in another direction so that they simply *do* not see? Are they without spiritual eyes so that they *cannot* see? Or are they merely stubborn and *will* not?

Does it clear up some of your confusion about those persons? Have you been praying for God to *give* His light to someone who is so conditioned by past environment or limited Biblical interpretation that his eyes are *blinded* to new truth? Or perhaps this person's eyes are blind because he has never received God's very first ray of light into the naturally darkened heart. God is always willing, eager to give His light. Perhaps you should change your prayer and begin to ask Him to open those "blinded" eyes to see the initial need of a Saviour. Perhaps you should ask Him to bring about some circumstance or insight that will crack up that high wall of early conditioning. We will devote an entire chapter to the deep problems that result from conditioning, but for now, consider it, at least, as one kind of semi-blindness.

Perhaps you have been asking God to give light to someone who simply is not ready for light on a certain area. Or who is just plain stubborn! This is a foolish prayer. God *is* always eager to give light, because He is the Light, and He is always eager to give Himself to anyone. Better start in this instance, to pray for some heart melting. Where there is undue stubbornness, I have found it generally accompanied by a hard heart somewhere in the picture. It may be the heart of the person who needs the prayed-for light, or it just could be your own heart.

One woman told me she had prayed for years for her husband, who had committed adultery, to become a Christian. Nothing happened. It was plain to me why nothing happened. This woman had not forgiven her husband. He was still a rascal to her, and it showed in her entire personality. She was "superior" to him. She sat in constant judgment upon him. How could God answer the prayer of a woman with her heart closed and calloused with condemnation and bitterness?

Before we look at some of the problems which result from *darkness,* it would be a good idea, I think, for us to realize that some who claim to be Christian, do act as though they are still in the dark. Only God really knows whether or not His life has invaded the life of a human being. This is not for us to decide. But it is for us to consider, if we are being realistic about the problems which surround persons like this and often touch us.

Any illustration here could easily slip into oversimplification, but it is generally true that Christians have some dark areas. One of the kindest Christian ladies I've ever met impressed me because she seemed never to condemn anyone. When I mentioned it to her, she laughed and said, "Well, before I draw any conclusions at all, I go for a long time believing that person is simply still in the dark in that area!"

I watched a well-meaning but heavy-handed evangelical brother slam the door of the Kingdom in the face of a Jewish actor several years ago. What this kind woman said helped me greatly. This sensitive, intelligent, hungry-hearted young actor was near the point of opening his blinded eyes to the true identity of the Messiah. Then one night, after the young man had turned in a beautiful performance on the program I was directing, the zealous "personal worker" variety Christian brother button-holed him in a corner of the studio, and Bible in hand, informed him that as a sinner he had no right to read the lines of Jesus Christ. "The very fact that you're an actor proves you're a child of the devil!" And then he proceeded to flip from page to page in his Bible, showing the embarrassed Jewish boy verse and chapter to back up his charges. And "charges" they were, too. He lashed out the wonderful Bible verses like a prosecuting attorney. He seemed to gloat when he found a verse that "proved" the young man was a sinner! Verses about sin in the Bible are there to give light to a man in darkness and not to beat him down. And surely not to swell the ego of a whirl-wind "personal worker." I watched the young, sensitive face harden. I felt my own heart break. I felt a little of the heart-break of God too. My own human nature wanted to rush across the studio and shake the preaching brother by the scruff of his neck and shout: "You're kicking a blind man for being blind! Don't you *see?*"

Then I checked myself. I was about to do exactly the same thing! This brother was in darkness, too, in the all-important area of the sensitized heart. I could not doubt that his own personal faith was in Jesus Christ as his Saviour, but without a doubt — if I really faced the *facts* — this man was in considerable darkness.

We must always face the facts. Then, we must make every careful attempt to understand these facts and to apply them to the situation at hand. Suppose God made no allowances at all for our blind spots? Our areas of darkness? Suppose the all-loving God did *not* "remember that we are dust!"

The Bible-thumping "personal worker" is only one example of the confusion which can result from semi-darkness. Most persons are not Bible thumpers. This requires a certain type of inflamed human ego. But we all have varying amounts of that "certain type of human ego" and only the Holy Spirit of God can give us the needed light to change our general approach to life. The true follower of Jesus Christ treads softly among other human beings, aware that the ground on which he walks is holy ground. This is not natural to most persons. It is supernatural. It is the result of revealed light from God Himself. If I am not careful, I can sit in high condemnation of the Bible thumpers! They are wrong, they are un-Christlike, but so am I when I condemn them.

How do I know this? Do I know it because I studied it in the Scriptures? Yes, in part this is how I know. I had to be willing to shed my deplorable spiritual ignorance which I brought with me into the Kingdom. I had to begin to hate my ignorance and to open my mind to new knowledge. I had to read and re-read the words of Jesus: "The Son of Man came not to condemn, but to save!"

But merely reading them, or merely re-reading them would not have dispelled my darkness and enabled me to face the facts about that offending brother, who frightened away the young man I hoped to see become a believer. I could have clenched my fist and repeated His words over and over that night, but my heart would not have basked in the *light* of its own dispelled darkness, as I experienced actual pity and concern instead of loathing for the man with the Bible in his hand.

Without a doubt, I had to abandon my ignorance and learn of Him, but my heart would have remained in *darkness*, if the Holy Spirit had not flooded it with His everlasting light!

Reasonably intelligent men and women can memorize Scripture and understand some of the principles of Kingdom living, *but* this intellectually acquired knowledge can remain a collection of hard facts.

When God shines His light into our darkness, *love* always comes with it! Christendom is well populated by men and women with "correct doctrine" and an impressive array of theological know-how. But only God knows how to flood a human heart with love.

When God gives light, He always gives love right along with it. This is inevitable, since God *is* love. He can give no authentic part of Himself without giving love. This, of course, is why only God could dare to sit in judgment upon the human heart. Only God could sort out the vagaries and shadows and horrors of the human heart and still go on loving that heart as He does.

So, one of the most disconcerting problems which result from spiritual darkness is met here: Weak and sinful men and women go about in semi-darkness "playing God" with other men and women who are as weak and sinful and helpless as we are! Christian men and women get hold of a few truths and attempt to do God's work for Him — in semi-darkness. Only God is full of light. Only God is love. Only God is God.

In her altogether provocative new book, *You Can Witness With Confidence* (Zondervan), Rosalind Rinker makes excellent use of a pungent quotation: "Real evangelism is one beggar telling another beggar where to find bread!"

If you feel strong and correct, look out! If you go about trying to set others straight according to your plumbline, God help you! And God help the others you are trying to "help."

One woman wrote, "My mother is a marvelous woman, but she is *right* about everything! I love her, but I simply can't live in the house with her and neither can my sister."

Only God is right about everything. Only God's plumbline falls straight, and only He has a right to use it. Unless we feel like helpless beggars, we are in at least semi-darkness!

If you approach a troubled person in the spirit of just another beggar who has found bread, God will stand a chance of getting both His light and His bread to that fellow beggar, just as He got it to you.

Lack of identification is one more real problem which results from spiritual *darkness*. More aptly, the lack of understanding the *reason* for identification. A Christian believes that God came down to our planet when Jesus was born in Bethlehem of Judea the first Christmas. The deity of Jesus Christ is one of the primary tenets of the Christian faith. In fact, it is the key. The identity of this Man from Nazareth is the cornerstone of faith to the Christian. This is the stone on which Jesus said He would build His church. When big, burly, eager Peter got hold of the truth from on high and declared: "Thou art the Christ, the Son of the living God!" Jesus said, in effect, "This is it. This is the central truth."

"If you have seen Me, you have seen the Father."

Orthodox Christians believe this. But how many of us are still in semi-darkness as to *why* God became a human being? Why did He so thoroughly *identify* with man? Why is it so important for us to be rid of our darkness here? Why must this great condescension of God be at least in part understood by us? Why do we dare not "accept" the deity of Christ as a "safe" doctrinal point and go on about our church work? Won't we go to heaven anyway when we die? Yes, this is not the point in question.

With all my being, I believe that people must come out of darkness on this point of God's identification, or they will miss most of the creativity of living the Christian life on this earth! God found it necessary to identify utterly with fallen man. Why? Nothing less than that would have melted my heart. Nothing less than that would have melted yours. The Divine-human equation would have been forever incomplete, if God had not come. Men can worship and fear the God of the Old Testament without knowing His true identity as it is *revealed* in the New Covenant. He can worship Him and fear Him and even obey Him, but man cannot return love except to another human being! Man's heart needs another heart to love, to which to respond. God knew this. He "created our hearts alike," the Psalmist wrote. He knew the wide variations among men's minds. God could not reveal Himself to fallen man through his mind, but He could do it through man's heart. And He did, in Jesus. If God and Jesus Christ are one and the same, then God incites love in His creatures. But the mere head knowledge that Jesus is the Son of God is not enough.

The Holy Spirit, whom Jesus said would teach us all things, must carry this shining truth into the deepest pockets of our darkened hearts.

If the problem of darkness on the part of a member of your church or family is causing problems for you, stop a moment to face the possible facts. Do these problem people really walk in the light of the knowledge of God's heart *as He revealed it in Jesus,* or do they merely hold the doctrinal belief in the deity of Christ?

If the problem of no communication between you and your child creates havoc in your house and heart, could it be that you, yourself, have not been lighted up from within on the *necessity for identification?* Are you really identifying with your child? Or are you sitting in remote judgment, explaining nothing, forgetting entirely how you felt at that age, and refusing to understand the complexities of the young?

What if God had remained on His throne, merely giving

us orders? What if He had gone on saying, as so many parents say, "Do it because I say to do it!"

Think. We must think. We must be quiet and think and weigh and interpret the facts. People who are in darkness cannot be expected to act as though they are in light! If you try to walk rapidly at night across the most familiar room in your house without turning on the light, the chances are you will stumble or even fall. Can you expect someone who is in total or semi-darkness not to do the same thing?

Think a long time about *darkness* and its inevitable consequences. Be realistic about it. Be realistic about those who are evidently still in it to some degree. Be realistic about your own dark places. And then give God the chance He longs to have. Light comes slowly at times. Don't expect Him to strike your collected problems of the years with a bolt of heavenly lightning and dispel them! God's tempo is always right, and He works as rapidly as we permit. But give yourself time, too. Time to think. Time to recognize just how much of the present problem could be due to someone's darkness.

"Wake up, sleeper, and rise from the dead, and Christ shall shine upon you!" Wake up and give yourself time to *think*.

Give yourself enough alert time to weigh the matter in His presence, always remembering that His primary concern is not merely to throw some new light on your current crisis in order to make life easier for you. His concern is to make you a whole person.

"The people who sat in darkness have seen a great light."

But we — these people — need to sit in that light and think, and sometimes learn how to see all over again. Light can be painful until our eyes grow accustomed to it. If we have sat in the darkness for a long time, we will need to learn again (maybe for the first time), "to walk in the light, as He is in the light."

6: The Problem of Extremism

6. The Problem of Extinction

6:

THE PROBLEM OF EXTREMISM

We have been thinking about the difference between viewing a problem in darkness and viewing the same problem in the light of God's own insight on the matter.

Without a doubt *light* makes all the difference. And God is just as willing to give you His understanding (light) on the personality problems of another person as He is to give you understanding of the Scriptures.

In Chapter 4, on the problems resulting from *ignorance,* we considered the meaning of the Biblical instruction that we are to "let that mind be in you which is in Christ Jesus." Surely, if we have the viewpoint of Christ, we have a realistic viewpoint. Surely, if we have the mind of Christ, we have a balanced mind. A balanced mind inevitably results in a balanced personality. If one's mind is *extreme* in any area, the total personality may become extreme.

It has been said that "Jesus Christ was all sanctity, but He was also all sanity." This is true. Jesus did not do eccentric things. He was balanced and poised and quiet at the center of His being. He understood how to relate values and He took the time to do so. He accepted people and situations *as they were,* not as His God-mind told Him they should be.

He always reckoned with man as helpless in his own strength, but He did not stop there. He related the weaknesses and inadequacies of every human personality with the tremendous potential of that personality when it was linked with the life of God through faith in Him.

No one ever shocked Jesus or threw Him for a loss. He "knew what was in man." He expected men to act like men. He did not expect a man who had not entered the Kingdom to act as though he had. He did not expect love from men with no love to give. He did not expect loyalty from Judas. He knew Judas. He knew the pressures of waiting for Jesus to reveal His Messiahship publicly, were too much for Judas' high-strung, impatient personality. Judas was an extremist!

Jesus knew this. As I wrote through the story of Jesus' life on earth with His disciples in my book, *Beloved World,* I became more and more convinced that Jesus understood thoroughly why Judas did what he did. It was no surprise to the Master that Judas' passion to be a part of the new Kingdom drove him to the action he took. Judas simply could not wait! I do not believe he was even figuratively the "incarnation of the devil." I believe Judas was a violent extremist, and there are still many such extremists among the followers of the Son of God.

Perfectionism is one of the most hazardous *extremes* one can encounter in a human personality. A broken-hearted gentleman said to me one day: "I know I'm full of faults, and it's a bitter pill that my wife is divorcing me. But honestly, Genie, no man could ever live up to her! I never was perfect and she was destroying us both trying to make me be what no man could be."

This man spoke a deep truth, not only about his wife, but about many wives. *Perfectionist* tendencies in a woman can create unmanageable false guilt in a man. There is no surer way to invite "the other" woman into the picture than to demand perfection of a husband. I do not need to be a wife to know this. It is simply a basic law of human nature. When a wife demands that her husband be "perfect," she loads him with false guilt and the most natural thing in the world is for him to find another woman who will accept him as he is. Human nature needs encouragement, not derision. And if a woman is a perfectionist, she will never be satisfied with her husband's behavior or personality, and inevitably she derides him. If her viewpoint is so far removed from God's viewpoint as to expect a man to be more than he is, she will not be able to do anything but run him down. He will never be what she expects and so unreality and chaos rule the house! There is room for *improvement* in every man — in every woman, for that matter, but no one can ever be "improved" enough to meet the high standards of the perfectionist.

The trouble which follows the disturbed wake of a perfectionist wife is not the only bad consequence of this type of extremism. Anyone who sets standards for others or for himself which are too high for attainment, is a havoc-maker.

I know of an excellent artist in his late thirties. He has been working almost literally night and day since he was in his teens, painting canvas after canvas — "perfecting" his technique for painting "light." This is altogether admirable in essence. No one ever becomes a great artist by instinct only. But this young man refuses to this day to show a single picture! The few authorities, including his teacher, who have seen his work are lyrical about it. According to the best, authentic judgment, he was ready to begin to show and sell his paintings years ago. Still he refuses. Still his parents support him. His parents or the few friends who haven't grown bored with his fanatic perfectionism. Most real artists have certain *extremes* in their personalities. Most great people tend to extremes of one sort or another, but with God (and this boy knows Christ), extremes can be controlled.

Most of us are convinced that this man — perhaps quite unconsciously — uses his *perfectionism* as an alibi for not taking the risk of his life's work being rejected by the public and the critics. As long as he rants and raves about the fact that he still "sees" more light than he can paint, as long as he continues to escape risk in the sanctuary of his art studio, he *is* safe from rejection. But he is "safe" from acceptance, too! His pictures should be hanging on the walls of churches and colleges and homes. They should be shared by those who would love them and appreciate them. But he cannot be convinced. His *extreme* is rank *perfectionism*.

Parents are often extremists with their children, and nothing can disrupt a child's needed sense of security more quickly. One mother confessed to me that she has no control over her children at all any more because she flies at them in a would-be disciplinary rage and the next hour, she is giving in to them on every score. Her husband is extreme in another way. He ignores the children for days or even weeks, particularly if he happens to be busy in a big church drive of some kind, and when he remembers them suddenly one day, it is usually with an extreme form of punishment in the back room. How stable could these children be, growing up in the confusion of such *extremes* in both parents? Both these parents are evangelical Christians. Both believe firmly in the fact that Christ lives in them! Neither will find the balance needed to become a good parent, however, until each one sees and recognizes the areas of his and her personality which are *extreme*. Any extreme area in our lives is obviously not under Christ's control!

He is all balance.

How is your *money* situation? More aptly, what is your attitude and behavior where your money is concerned? Here, two *extremes* prevail among both men and women. Both can cause equal personality distortion and downright trouble. I know of a refined, otherwise lovable lady in her middle seventies, who (in spite of a fairly fat savings account and a good sized pile of stock certificates, plus a regular income from five apartments), is so stingy with her money she won't wash her dishes but once a day! She is saving a handful of pennies on her water bill and a few granules of detergent. If this kind of quirk ended with her household "thrift," it would probably not do much damage, since she lives alone. But recently, she changed churches because the church she had attended for years launched a building program! When asked why she was hanging on for dear life to her money, she snapped: "Why, to leave to my son!"

Her son is one of the wealthiest lawyers in town.

The other side of the money "coin" is just as troublesome. This is the side I know well from past experience. Until I became a follower of Jesus Christ, I was more adept than anyone I have discovered since, at living *beyond* my income. As a single woman, this only inconvenienced my creditors and my faithful parents. But it marked my personality, just as surely as the personality of the stingy woman who polishes her pennies, is marked. I had no respect for money and little balance in the other areas of my life. I was extravagant with compliments and led people to think they meant much more to me than anyone could in those days. My flamboyance with money made me a flamboyant person, and I believe vice versa. The results were just as predictable as if I had been too penurious, and just as devastating.

It is my understanding that much of the friction in families is due to the tendency of either parent or both, to live beyond the family income. For concrete good advice and genuine help on this problem, I wholeheartedly recommend an interesting and positive little book titled: *Here's How To Succeed With Your Money,* by George M. Bowman (Moody Press). This man is an authentic Christian and managing money is his business.

"A father of five children took his own life early yesterday because he could no longer face his mounting debts."

I just copied that from a clipping on my desk.

Here is the other *extreme* in an excerpt from another news item: "An elderly man, believed by his neighbors to be extremely poor, died today, leaving a fortune of two hundred thousand dollars in securities and cash hidden in his unpainted shack where he had lived for thirty-five years."

Which *extreme* is yours where money is concerned? Either one is controllable by the Lord who loves you.

Work is one of God's greatest gifts to us. Life on this earth is only half-life when one has no constructive work to do. But here, too, we become *extreme.* The greed for money is not the only reason some people over-work.

A woman told me some months ago, between horrified sobs, that her husband (a Christian leader) finally admitted to her that he worked such long hours in his particular religious field, because he preferred the peace and quiet of his office to being at home with her!

I understand the *extremism* of over-loving work. Perhaps I should say of "escaping" into work. Some of you have read in my other books that I have to surrender the whole effort, each time I leave my writing to pack for a speaking trip. True. Still true. I will have to do this at about the halfway point in this book, in fact. There is certainly nothing wrong with a writer loving to write. In fact, unless one does, one had better quickly look elsewhere for a new profession. *But* I must watch myself constantly here and lean heavily on the fact that I now write in the good discipline of a partnership! I am no longer writing for myself. The Creator is my partner now. And just as He can keep the creative ideas flowing, so He can keep me balanced where my love for writing is concerned.

A friend told me years ago (and unfortunately it is still true) that she dreads to see her mother visit her because the mother does nothing during the entire visit but wash walls and scrub floors and clean windows in her daughter's home. The daughter is a good housekeeper. This is not the point. The point is that her mother (a "sound" Christian) is *unsound* in the work department.

"I made up my mind," my friend declared, "that when I was married and had a house of my own, it would never own me the way Mother's house always owned her. My husband grits his teeth and bears it while Mother's with us, but the minute we put her back on the train, we all put our feet up on the cushions and throw the evening paper around the house and whoop like Indians!"

I know this mother, too. She is a lovely person — attractive, well dressed, refined, sincere. But it is utterly impossible to converse with the poor woman about anything but *houses!* She has been so extreme on this point all her life that she has simply not had time to read a book. She gives mine away (bless her) as gifts, but she has never read even one of them herself.

Highly *opinionated* persons are also troublesome *extremists.* Most persons with active brains have strong opinions about the things which matter to them. This is normal. Strong opinions are valuable things. As James said, "A double-minded man is unstable in all his ways." But there is a gigantic difference between having strong opinions and *being opinionated.* The difference is in the attitude of the heart. A person with strong opinions can be disagreed with and there is no damage done on either side. But the *opinionated* person strikes fire!

This is another area of *extremism* where God has had a big job to do with me. I hope I have made some progress, but for most of my life, I had the aggravating habit of dismissing entire areas of discussion with a dogmatic, "Oh, that's simply not so!" In other words — "I'm right. Let's not even discuss it further!"

Such extremism is usually due to a basic lack of humility. If you find yourself flaring (even inwardly) when someone disagrees with you on one of your pet theories or doctrines, run to God! You may be right in your theory or doctrine, but you are not right in your emotional balance. Your *opinion* owns you, just as surely as my friend's mother's housework owned her.

In this same area of *extremism,* there is also the other side of the "coin." Just as much confusion can result from a namby-pamby person who seemingly has no opinions of her own. Usually, a person like this has trouble even making a decision, much less sticking to it. I know a woman who appears to be humble, because she can take criticism without batting an eye. I admired and even envied this trait in her until I realized it was due mainly to the fact that she had very few opinions even about *herself.* She did not flare at criticism because she wasn't sure that the other person might be entirely right and she entirely wrong. She took compliments with the same unbatted eye. The same conclusion can be drawn. She is not flattered or even particularly pleased because she isn't sure who's right about that either.

We could fill a book with *extremes*. No need to do this. They all spring from a basically *eccentric* personality. And the solution here is the same one I discovered (thank God!), by the time I was three years old as a Christian, and writing my first little book, *Discoveries*. Jesus Christ is the *weight* — the Rock. When He, Himself, is in the center of our lives, we are balanced. When we put anything else in the center — anything, even something pertaining to Him, like doctrine, church work, or even the Bible — He (the weight) is pushed to the margin and we tip! We become *ec*-centric. Off-center.

Or we begin to live our lives in fragments. In short, we literally "go to pieces." What can keep us centered down? What can keep us integrated, bound together into a balanced, whole personality? Only hour-by-hour contact with Jesus Christ.

Because "He is Himself, before all, and *in Him*, all things are framed together." In Him, in this Christ who lives in us, all of the fragments of our personalities, and all our *extremism* can be held together. Balanced.

If you have begun to see your extremes, don't despair. Give thanks. As soon as we have seen a need in His Presence, the need has begun to be met!

"Before they call, I will answer; while they are yet speaking, I will hear."

God has been ready a long, long time to make us balanced human beings.

7: The Problem of Conditioning

7:

THE PROBLEM OF CONDITIONING

According to the dictionary, the word *conditioning,* as we will be considering it in this chapter, means a state of being "limited or restricted in thought or conception."

We are all *conditioned.* It would be impossible for a woman to grow to adulthood without any conditioning. This does not mean that all conditioning is bad. Please have this straight in your mind. But the extent to which we have allowed ourselves to be permanently limited or restricted by conditioning is more important and more closely related to many of our everyday problems than we suspect.

As a simple starting example, you may be a "dyed-in-the-wool" Republican. Perhaps your parents and grand-parents were Republicans before you. You have heard nothing but blasts against all Democrats and so your political *conditioning* snaps your mind shut on Election Day. The danger comes, of course, when early conditioning is so strong that the person's mental choices may be not only twisted from right to wrong, but hampered or even cut off. If you look down your nose at all Democrats or Republicans, as the case may be, how can you weigh the facts clearly before you vote? We get right back to our original premise — the *real issues* are often hard to see. Impossible, in fact, unless we recognize the results of our *conditioning.*

I happen to be a Republican by registration. I used to be a thoroughly *conditioned* one. So conditioned, in fact, that after I became a Christian in 1949, I had a dreadful time learning to pray for our Democratic President!

Does this make you smile? Me too. But the principle involved is a tragic explanation of much of our general daily distress. *Right conditioning* can guide and govern our thinking and behavior, but it becomes *wrong conditioning* when it builds a prison wall around our minds.

A friend observed the effects of wrong conditioning among the children of a Christian family close to her. It so happened these people were Swedish and lived in a Chicago suburb on a street with other immigrant families, some of whom were Italian. One day my friend heard the children, when they were quite small, making fun of the "wops" down the block. When she inquired, they smirked and said, "Oh, they're different from us! They're *Italians!*"

One of the children dared to begin to think for herself when she reached high school. Years later my friend overheard her say, "Mother, we were wrong about Italian people. They're just like us!"

This unfortunate brand of conditioning does go on in Christian homes. Among Americans. Among American Christians. The Swedes stay in their own little safety areas among themselves, the Italians in theirs, the Baptists in theirs, and the Methodists in theirs. Truly *Christian* conditioning never creates anxiety over stepping outside little false safety areas. Truly Christian influence never creates either anxiety or false safety areas! Jesus said, "If the Son shall make you free, you shall be free indeed!"

Conditioning becomes a real complicator of human relationships when one follows one's conditioning blindly, without ever having thought through the real issues involved. True Christian conditioning never leads to a locked-up mind, afraid to face issues realistically.

I am an American. I have been conditioned to being an American. With America at war, it was natural for me to feel anger and dislike toward America's enemies. But why? Did I really know why I believed the United States to be in the right? Does my heart stretch with patriotism at the sound of our national anthem and the sight of our beautiful flag simply because I was taught to feel that way? Or am I really stirred in the depths of my own individual being because I truly believe *for myself* in the content of the United States Constitution? For that matter, have I ever taken the time to find out what's in our Constitution? Have I looked into the *facts* involved in being an American? Or am I just haughty with foreigners because we dole out so much money to the countries they love as much as I love mine?

I am an evangelical Christian. Why? Because I was conditioned to be? No, I was not. I am an evangelical Christian because I am convinced that God and Jesus Christ are One and this conviction alone keeps me interested in doing all I can to let this glorious fact be known.

Are you an evangelical Christian? If you are, why are you? Is it because everyone you know is also?

I want to share a portion of a recent letter with you, but first, check yourself and your conditioning against these two tests: (1) Has your religious conditioning made you *afraid?* (2) Has it created *prejudice* in you?

Both *fear* and *prejudice* are anti-Christian. Therefore, if your religious conditioning has made you fearful and prejudiced, I urge you to discuss the ways in which this is so with God right now.

In the light of what you have probably found out from Him, if you took time to listen, how would you answer this letter?

"I am facing the first real crisis of my married life. My husband and I felt God prompted our marriage five years ago and until my husband's senior year at the university where he studied law, we were blissfully happy. About that time (two years ago now) he began to become restless with the church we attended. It has always been my church and he joined it when we were married, although he had come to know God personally in another denomination. Now he seems to think the people in my church are narrow. We are a fairly small denomination and very orthodox. I do not mean to imply my husband is not orthodox in his basic beliefs. He is. But for months now, we have had bitter quarrels because of certain forms of worship in the little church. He also objects to certain prohibitions I have always obeyed as a matter of training. I am, frankly, *frightened* half to death!

"Things have gotten so bad now that he is threatening to stop attending church altogether if I don't agree to move to another church with him. He doesn't have any particular choice of a church, but just wants one which he describes as 'a place where a man can think!' I agree that our group in my church is somewhat old fashioned. But I honestly don't know how I could bear to change churches now. I know I would be suspicious of everything any other minister said. I would never feel at home the way I always have in our present church. I hate to face it, but I must admit, I guess, that I'm just plain *prejudiced* against the others.

"Please help me. I am beside myself with worry."

Here is an example of *religious conditioning* which is about to break up an otherwise strong relationship. The sincere young lady who wrote the letter is terrified of the whole idea, but her last few lines showed me that she *is* daring to think a little in her own right before God. There is one encouraging line in the entire letter: "I must admit, I guess, that I'm just plain *prejudiced* against the others."

Some self-knowledge is breaking through despite her strong, sentimental and emotional *conditioning*. First of all, I have no doubts that this woman could go contentedly on in that little church. The point here is in no way to criticize her small denomination. She didn't mention it, and even if she had, this is definitely *not* the point. The point is that God created individuals, each with the tremendous potential of walking individually with Him. Evidently her husband is not in rebellion against God or the Christian faith. He simply has begun to think for himself and feels stifled in the atmosphere which is so home-like to her.

Should this marriage be allowed to go on the rocks because of this girl's rigid religious *conditioning?* I think not. God has made her and her husband one flesh. Her husband's rebellion is not a foolish kind. A man has a right to think. She should be rejoicing that, although he followed her meekly into the little church at first, he is now beginning to think like the head of his house. His thinking is not taking him away from God, but he can get away if her *fear* and *prejudice* resulting from her own conditioning keeps God surrounded with quarreling!

The young wife ended her letter by saying she is searching her heart for the answer. I suggest she search the Scriptures, too. They are not "conditioned" by anything but God's love for both her and her husband! And the scripture I suggest is not the obvious one about the wife being submissive to her husband. This is good, but if she gritted her teeth and went with him to another church without seeing the *real issues* involved, the end result could be just as disastrous as it is now while he grits his teeth and continues on with her.

I suggest that she re-read what Jesus Himself had to say in the story of the woman at the well in John 4:21-24.

"Believe me, woman, the time has come when you shall worship the Father neither merely in this mountain nor merely in Jerusalem. . . . The hour comes — and is now here — when genuine worshipers shall worship the Father in spirit and truth; for the Father is looking for such as His worshipers. God is a Spirit and His worshipers must worship in spirit and truth."

Could we paraphrase that a bit without changing any of its meaning?

"Believe me, woman, the time has come when you shall worship the Father neither merely in your little church nor merely in another. . . . The hour comes—and is now here — when genuine worshipers shall worship the Father in spirit and truth; for the Father is looking for such as His worshipers who attend church for His sake (for love's sake) and who have finally caught on that God *is* a Spirit and so it is forever possible for His worshipers to worship Him anywhere without limitation so long as their own spirits are involved with truth!"

A man must be allowed to think. A woman must be allowed to think. When our past conditioning blocks peace as is the case with this couple, the conditioning must be re-conditioned with the free Spirit of love Himself!

Perhaps we should look squarely at freedom for a moment. In no way does it mean license. You have heard this before, I'm sure. What does freedom really mean? Rather than attempting the (to me) unrealistic task of making a long list of do's and don't's in order to define *freedom* and *license,* why not be realistically Christian about it as Jesus was? He simply said, "Follow Me!" He *is* love. Our God is not remote and undiscoverable. He has already fully revealed Himself in Jesus of Nazareth. We can know Him as *love Himself.* There is no rigidity in love. "God *is* love." Therefore, if this God, this Son, shall make us free, isn't real freedom the state of living which never cuts across the heart of love? Real love is never rigid, but neither does it compromise itself. If I really love you, I won't even want to cause you to stumble. And if we live lives separated (not necessarily from a few *things*) but from *anything* that is opposed to Holy Love, we are being free, authentic, creative followers of Jesus Christ.

My publishers sent a collection of reviews of my two books *Woman to Woman* and *Strictly Personal* to me last week. When I found a free evening, I sat down and read them all carefully. With all of me I believe my critics are the "unpaid guardians of my soul." Many of the reviews (all written by outstanding Christian men and women) were most generous. Some, however, openly stated that I did not give doctrine enough emphasis. This interests me greatly, because in both books under consideration, I repeated and repeated and repeated my own life conviction that the one doctrine set down by Jesus Himself *is essential.* On the day Peter caught the Word from heaven that his Master was "the Christ, the Son of the Living God," Jesus said He would build His church on that fact! Throughout all my books this truth rings loud and clear. But my conscientious critics did not recognize their *particular* doctrinal emphasis couched in the language with which they are familiar and so due to this *pre-conditioning,* they thought me swampy.

I thoroughly understand this. Since I do not pretend to be an authority on the doctrines of the Christian church, I stick to what I know and what I know to be central for everyone. All these people would have agreed with me in the main. I just didn't sound "familiar."

Not only must we check the effects of our conditioning, we must accept the fact in each other that we *are* all conditioned. I do not happen to have a religious background. I am a Christian by convincement only. Of course, I will express myself according to my own conditioning, as they will express themselves according to theirs. I have found persons from opposing doctrinal schools believing that I agree with both! We find what we are most familiar with. We are *afraid* not to find it most of the time. But you who have been conditioned to the "language of Zion" must be careful to remember that I was not and look for my real meaning. I must do the same with you. We must both double-check our conditioning in honest attempts to keep our communication lines open to those who are still outside. And we must check it constantly, to be sure it is not creating either *fear* or *prejudice* in us. You must not be prejudiced against me if I do not express myself your way, and I must not be prejudiced toward you if you do not express your thinking my way. Neither must we allow ourselves to become *afraid* of any members of God's own household.

We must all remember Jesus' startling statement about the man with the beam in his eye. Above all, our Lord longs to have us face the real issues on which we can unite and let the specks of difference blow away in the high, strong wind of His great love for us all.

There is only one kind of *conditioning* which can cause no unheavenly limitations or restrictions, and that is the conditioning of love.

"This is My instruction," Jesus said, "that you love one another as I have loved you."

We are conditioned by what we have done in the past, and by what we go on doing, and Jesus is still saying: "Continue ye in My *love*."

8: The Problem of Busyness

8:

THE PROBLEM OF BUSYNESS

If I had planned the chapters of this book on the "popularity" of the problems, *busyness* would have headed the list.

Most people are just too busy. This is a point for quick agreement, but the subtle danger involved in our *busyness* is that most of us never stop to realize that in most cases we can do something about it!

Like the harrassed young mother whose story I told you in the first chapter of this book, we tend to look wildly and unrealistically in every other direction for the cause of our trouble. Most of us feel like helpless victims where our work and activity schedules are concerned. For five or six years, this was entirely true of me.

Then one day, when I had actually fallen asleep on someone's sofa in the middle of a conversation, I began to take stock.

What was actually important? How much of this activity was God actually instigating? How much of it was the consequence of my own bad judgment, and how much was simply to keep people liking me? How much of it was guided by the Holy Spirit within me? What was really gained that evening I fell asleep during what to me was no longer "sweet fellowship"?

Every day and every evening on my desk calendar for

the years 1950 through 1955 is black with engagements. I know, because I just dug out these old calendars and checked. But I also leafed through 1956 and on up to the present time. There is something down for every *day*, but now, many of the *evenings* are blank! Unless I am writing, or speaking, most of my evenings are spent reading or listening to records. I had to be willing to be misunderstood by some hypersensitive "friends," but they have accepted me now as either eccentric or sensible, and I fully expect to live ten years longer on this earth.

I do not mean that I never entertain in my home or visit friends. I do. But I have faced the fact that I simply do not have the energy or mental stability to lead (1) a busy social life, (2) speak to a different group every night, (3) handle an always top-heavy correspondence, (4) keep a long distance travel schedule, (5) attend board meetings — and with a last gasp, write books!

It is normal for a new Christian to get wound up in a hectic life of Kingdom-busyness. But no one should be content with remaining a "new Christian." *Maturity* is the good goal here, and real maturity includes developing *judgment*.

Over and over again we hear of earnest Christian leaders having breakdowns due to overwork. I cannot believe this is God's idea for anyone. I do fully understand that it is just as easy for a man or woman to overwork in the religious field as in business — perhaps easier, since the Christian is always expected to go the "second mile." This interpretation of the "second mile" is not what Jesus meant, however. He spoke of the attitude of man's heart in the Sermon on the Mount. The fact remains, we as Christians place this impossible burden of over-busyness on each other, by not facing the real issues. Daily my mail brings two or more letters which begin:

"Dear Miss Price, I know you already carry an overloaded schedule, *but* —"

I recently heard a typical "fan" type lady sigh and say, "Oh, I was so *blessed* when I heard So and So sing the other night. That dear man swayed on his feet he was so tired! He is spending himself for God!"

Mr. So and So couldn't have been singing his best in that condition, let's face it. And there is nothing in my Bible which tells me I am to "spend" myself for God. As I understand it, I am to *live* for Him, so that my life presents a balanced, sane, alert picture of what the human life can be when it is linked with His life.

A dear friend told me with tears in her eyes not long ago that it had been over three months since she and her husband and their children had spent an evening at home together. She had hopes during the Christmas holidays, but they came and went and even on Christmas Eve, they had to go to church and after that the children had to attend some sort of young people's service or be thought slackers.

"What can we do?" she moaned. "I can *feel* my children growing away from their father and me. Even my husband and I can't find time to be alone except late at night when we are both too exhausted to do anything but tumble into our beds and sleep!"

This is what one woman did when God got her quiet long enough for a good talk with Him. I will try to reconstruct her story as she told it: "Things went along at our house much the same as they always had, except *I* suddenly found myself unable to cope with them anymore. At least they seemed to be going along the same. My younger children took me rather philosophically, as young children seem able to manage, but daily, I could see the communication between my fourteen-year-old and myself breaking down. I know growing boys sometimes get in a corner alone for a year or two, but this was more serious than that. My son and I actually had real arguments, and they never ended in understanding — just more lack of communication. He was my first-born and my heart ached over him, but every time a problem arose, I flew at him just as irrationally as he flew at me! Soon, I saw the communication lines weakening between my husband and me, too. He never argued with me—he's too kind and sensitive—

but he began to avoid discussions with me, and I felt more and more isolated. The general state of my own personality alarmed me. The warping had begun in earnest. I still had 'communication' (at least I called it that) with my younger children, and so I took it all out by over-disciplining them. More trouble followed, of course. They began to feel insecure because one day I punished unduly and the next day I'd try to compensate by spoiling them. I became dead sure my husband and my son were pulling away from me into a world of their own! This only made me more frantic. Oh, things went on — I kept at my housework (never finishing), did my own cooking, mending, laundry, and every night and some afternoons, there was something going on at our church. I was on umpteen committees, and then I was elected to an office in the PTA. I probably went along as long as I did because by nature, I'm a sound sleeper. When I began to lie awake all night until 4:00 A.M. I grew frantic. One morning I threw the alarm clock across the room and burst into tears.

"The upshot of the whole thing — I fell, running downstairs late starting breakfast, and landed in the hospital with an injured back and a real breakdown! Lying there day after day for weeks on my hospital bed, God had a chance, at last, to get my attention. Gently, gradually, He helped me see that I had allowed myself to get involved in more things than any woman could expect herself to handle. I had felt like a martyr, but God showed me I had really been a fool. My family visited me every day at the hospital, but consciously or unconsciously, they treated me — not like 'a great mother who had gone down filling her obligations to God and her family' — but like a problem child!

"They were right. I *was*. Finally I told my husband the whole thing. He wept a little for joy, too, and said he had also come to see how wrong he had been. Then and there we both promised God we would begin to use the wisdom He promises to give anyone who asks for it.

"One of the added benefits of my 'coming to myself'

came one day while I was still in the hospital. The minister of one of the other local churches dropped into my room to chat with me briefly. He stayed two hours and surprised both himself and me by pouring out his heart's problems, too! The same thing had happened at his house. In fact, he and his wife had definitely decided to separate. Yes, they still loved each other, but they both stayed so exhausted, it had been a long time since either of them had shown love to the other. This man and his wife joined my husband and me in making some changes. Of course, we all had to be willing to be misunderstood by some of the church people, and we were! But this minister and his wife are making a go of things now, and so are we at our house because we are *not* victims of *busyness* any longer. After all, this is still a free country! A man and woman can still say 'no.' And God is so eager to help us sort things out."

That night, after I spoke, this woman's teen-aged son stopped by the table where I was autographing books. The boy did not know his mother had talked to me at all.

"Thanks very much for your message, Miss Price," he said brightly. Then he looked at his beaming mother and grinned. "You're almost as smart as my mother!"

Communication lines were back up full force between those two. They were back up, however, only because this mother had stopped long enough to let God get through to her!

Frequently I am asked, "How am I going to get organized so I can get my work finished?"

Who can answer this question but you?

I can only assure you that, first of all, God wants you to be realistic about *you* and your obligations. Most of us are such egotists we expect far, far too much of ourselves. We accept offices and obligations beyond our strength and our ability to organize. If you are not "organized" by nature — if you tend to be haphazard at best — then don't try to remedy this situation by taking on still more work! You will only make things worse than ever. Accept yourself *as* you are and *where* you are.

Learning to be an orderly person is a slow process for most of us. And unless for some reason, you have no control over your life at all, you should begin to organize by *eliminating* everything possible to eliminate.

If your friends and fellow church members don't understand, it won't be the first time. But how do you know you couldn't start something valuable in your group by admitting to them that you feel guilty about your over-busyness? Nine times out of ten, they do, too. Ask their understanding and cooperation with you as you sincerely attempt to rescue your life from its present whirl. If you are criticized after honesty of this kind, skip it. Don't fall into the trap of false guilt.

I am convinced that most women are disorganized simply because they are trying to pack more into one 24-hour period than is possible. We never get through when we tackle too much to begin with. Then we feel guilty, and it is, if we are facing facts — false guilt.

It is almost impossible for an alcoholic to say "no." This is due mainly because he or she feels basically guilty at all times for being an alcoholic. When an alcoholic is sober, he or she is the easiest person to impose upon! I know a man who, before his conversion to Christ, was a real alcoholic. He is a fairly balanced Christian now — except for the fact that he still cannot say "no." The pattern of *doing* to try to make up for not *being* has been with him for so long, he is still trapped in it most of the time. He is no longer drinking, but he is mistreating his body and his mind and neglecting his family because he *never stops working!*

If we are honest, much of what we do, we do so that people will like us.

"We just don't think we'll ever forgive you if you refuse the presidency of the Missionary Guild again!"

Oh, yes they will. If God has convinced you by the very circumstances of your life and the jumpy state of your nerves, that someone else should take the load this year, you can trust the ladies to Him! If they don't forgive you, the guilt they are attempting to heap on you is *falsely* based, so forget it.

A woman's *ego* often pushes her into a whirlwind life of busyness, too. If you are capable, and if the ladies adore you and heap compliments on your pretty head every time you teach the class or preside at the circle meeting, just be wary. It is easy to mistake the voice of flattery for the voice of God. Especially if you've been busy for so long, there hasn't been a really quiet time to hear God speak.

It could be that you're not too busy. Some women aren't busy enough. Either excess can cause multiple troubles. One thing sure, no woman is her balanced best, no woman can think clearly and make wise decisions when she's physically and nervously exhausted. And still woman after woman chastises herself, pleads with God in prayer, and wonders why her temper doesn't vanish like an April snowflake, when she only needs to slow down! Woman after woman blames her husband or her children when their communication breaks down, and all the time, she is perhaps just too exhausted to communicate.

Excessive *busyness* affects single women as well as housewives. The whole atmosphere of a small business office changed when the Christian woman, who was office manager, finally tallied up her score before God. This took some doing. She had fired three new typists and a file clerk the month before God got at her with the reminder that she could not expect to have patience and show love and understanding toward those who worked under her as long as she was running every night to either a library board meeting, a church function or a fellowship meeting! She legislated quiet nights at home for herself. Among them were reading nights, music nights, or just nights to relax and watch TV. She began to go to sleep before midnight, and she got up half an hour earlier so there was time to enjoy the sun in her small apartment during breakfast. Soon a "new" woman was arriving at the office, and with her, a new atmosphere.

I now keep my "reading nights" as definitely as I keep speaking engagements. This is not unspontaneous, it is creative. I now feel somewhat true to myself. My relationship with God is much more meaningful than when I was exhausting myself in "full time service." When I "give" now, I have something to *give*.

True, most Christians are over-busy with church activities. I realize this presents a real problem for both minister and flock. However, recently I have spoken with several pastors who share my concern over the fact that Christians are just too busy to take advantage of the *rest* Jesus promised to His people. These men, in some instances, are planning and setting aside "family nights." *Not* family nights at the church — but family nights at home! One man urges his people every Sunday to keep one night free that week for rediscovering each other within the family circle.

These are wise, wise men. Their people are receiving wise counsel. The voice of God is always speaking to us, always trying to get our attention. But His voice *is* a "still, small voice," and we must at least slow down in order to listen.

9: The Problem of Competition

9:

THE PROBLEM OF COMPETITION

In the next chapter we will attempt the somewhat gigantic task of showing how the eight problems treated in Chapters 2 through 9 actually affect human relationships. I would not dare end this list of basic human problems, however, without an honest look at the *problems of competition,* perhaps one of the most unrecognized of all the complicators of daily life.

During the years when I lived with Ellen Riley Urquhart, the dear friend who led me to Christ, it took quite awhile for me to see that many of the problem areas we experienced with certain people, were created because these people insisted upon putting Ellen and me in *competition* with each other.

"Oh, Ellen's all right, I guess, but Genie's my favorite of the two!"

"I know Genie's the one who writes the books etc., but Ellen's the one I like best!"

Thank God this did not put us in competition with each other as far as *we* were concerned. The ill effects came as a result of the competition between us in the minds of these people. If Ellen had not recognized the situations as downright *competition,* however, I as a new Christian, would have really been confused.

The very definition of the word *competition* explains a

lot of the problem. According to the dictionary, *competition* is "a contest between rivals." How peaceful would our home have been if Ellen and I had allowed these unrealistic attitudes to make us "rivals"?

What's the situation in your house? If someone from outside is not "putting you into competition" with one another, are you doing it to yourselves?

"My husband does all the praying at our house. I know I am not forced to keep still, but it's his attitude that stops me. He just assumes that I'm no match for him when it comes to praying (and I guess I'm not), but there is such a feeling of inferiority in me, I just sit there and let him do it all. My children need to hear me pray for them, I know. But I don't. Not aloud. It's just another place where the rivalry between my husband and me goes on getting worse and worse."

This woman did see the real issue. It must be terrifying to wake up to the realization of this kind of competition between parents of children. Between any two persons, for that matter. Particularly between Christians.

Another letter disclosed this all too common contest between rivals. "I know the choir of a church is supposed to be the civil war battle-ground! Our choir is surely a good example. And I'm right in the middle of it every time. For years, I've been the soprano soloist. Now, a somewhat younger woman joined our church upon her marriage to one of our bachelor members, and she's a soprano too! Is it right for the director to give her more solos than he gives me, just because she's new? Honestly, Miss Price, I'm getting so I can't sing a note, I'm so full of resentment over all this. Should I leave the choir for good?"

Of course, I advised her go to the Lord Himself with her real problem. As so often happens, this dear lady was not facing the real issue. The real issue was not who should sing all the solos on a Sunday morning. The real issue was her jealousy and resentment. I could say nothing about the newcomer to the choir, because she was not the one who wrote to me.

Jealousy and resentment and feelings of inferiority and superiority are only a few of the bad fruits of the wrong kind of *competition*.

As long as one competes *toward a goal* with a constructive attitude, the competitive effort is creative. It is when the competitive spirit so takes over that we become personally involved and emotionally off-base, that chaos follows. *Competition* nibbles at the basic peace of God's people like an energetic band of termites, and still most of us fail to recognize it for what it is. And on it goes unhampered, wrecking relationships and dreams.

Someone told recently of having called the home of a local minister, hoping to talk for a few minutes about a problem with the minister's wife, who had a reputation as a counselor with women. The minister answered the telephone, since his wife was not at home. Would he have a spare moment to advise this woman?

"No, ma'am, not on your life!" he replied curtly. "My wife's the advice-giver around here. I stay strictly out of her territory!"

The woman who wanted advice, wisely did not call back. She sensed the unhealthy *competition* between this man and woman and went to another source.

Ruinous competitive spirit is, of course, not limited to the activities of Christendom. Something so innocent-seeming as a Garden Club competition can bring forth prickly consequences.

Just before Christmas this past year, I happened to be trying to do some research in the library of a small southern town. Unfortunately, for my concentration, the library was also small, and I had selected the day set aside for the ladies of the local Garden Club to bring their Christmas arrangements for judging!

One after another they came, arrangements in hand, their efforts all loudly praised by the breezy librarian, not ten feet from where I was trying to work.

Then a rather intense, smartly dressed young matron came bearing her styro-foam creation, replete with nodding locally grown poinsettias and pine.

"Oh, isn't that a dahling creation!" the librarian caroled, heartily. "Let's just put it right here in the center of this big, long, side shelf where it's going to show and show and show!"

The moment crackled. This lady was not going to leave its location up to anyone! For twenty minutes there was a chaos of movement and trying and viewing and fluttering and fluttering. There simply were no "showy" spots left in the library lounge!

"I hate competition anyway!" the disappointed matron snapped, as she scooped up her creation and departed, almost in tears.

Did she really hate competition? No, she hated being bested in it. Obviously, she had entered it willingly, but then her emotions took over. She had not merely worked out an attractive arrangement to enter in the local competition, she had herself become competitive! I'm sure her husband and children paid dearly for this later on that day.

The chaos of competition can so take over the human personality that some people simply cannot bear to fail. We should all be taught how to fail, because most of us do not know.

I remember clearly one evening at the home of friends in a Chicago suburb several years ago. I was speaking later to the women's group in their church, but our dinner conversation hummed happily around the two boys, aged 13 and 15. They were each competing that night in the wrestling finals at school. For months they had trained and dieted and waited for that night. Neither boy ate much (at least not much for teen-agers), but both were confident they would win their respective matches.

When their mother and I returned from the meeting, we were greeted at the front door by the father with one arm thrown happily around each son. "You won!" we shouted. "Nope," the younger boy said, still smiling, "we both lost."

Their father had spent time teaching them how to fail. That night I know he was prouder than if they had won hands down! The competition had been keen. Both boys really tried. Both boys almost succeeded. But there were no tears, no alibis, no complaints about the referee. The competition had been a healthy one, and their emotions were strengthened rather than scarred.

In direct contrast, I have appeared on the same program at large Christian youth rallies where young men and women, older than these two boys, have fled the stage weeping bitterly when they "went down" trying to recite strings of Bible verses from memory. One boy shouted from the wings of the big theatre where the rally was being held, "I'll never come back to this lousy meeting again!"

Inner chaos from allowing the competition to *possess* him.

Not much needs to be written to call attention to the already well known fact that even Christian men and women strain their nerves and their bank accounts to the breaking point, trying to keep up with the Christian Joneses.

Churches are supposed to be places where people who love Jesus Christ go to worship Him. Churches are also places where some women go to "perform" for the "glory of their new outfits." Missionary chairmen of women's groups are supposed to be women with a real heart burden for those less fortunate than themselves. Usually they are. At least one missionary chairman confessed to me, however, that she had refused to go to the spring luncheon to give her report on the group's missionary activities because her husband had refused to allow her to buy a new spring outfit. "I knew all the others on the program would have one, and I just couldn't face it!"

Another woman wept at me for almost an hour because her husband, an official in their church, had not only stopped attending church himself, but refused to drive her because his automobile was four years old and the man who held the other high church office had a new Cadillac!

Extremes? Perhaps. But just as some diseases reach advanced stages because they are not arrested early, so can the spirit of competition infect the human personality until it is in an advanced state of chaos.

There is more painful inner chaos twisting in the hearts of more women because it is still "a man's world," than most of us will admit. I am certainly not going to involve myself in the futile business of discussing whether or not it *is* still "a man's world." I am a single woman and have always been. To me, it is neither a man's world, nor a woman's world. It is God's world, and there is room for both varieties of His creatures. Healthy competition between the sexes, particularly in the area of work, is fine with me. In fact, it stimulates me. But it can, and does (as in other areas), turn to bitter, unhealthy, life-damaging rivalry.

I learned recently of the early days of one of God's still very useful women, whose personality was apparently permanently marked by the harsh competition that had sprung up between her and a Christian brother with whom she worked. The Christian "brother," in an evident attempt to keep her in her place (i.e. beneath him — fearing her brilliant mind), berated her so often publicly, that her natural humiliation turned to venom in her heart. Now people say she is a good person to give a wide berth! She had been so hurt by this ugly *competition* in her youth, she still is prone to lash out with the same competitive attitude toward anyone who blocks her way.

(This type of competition, of course, need not be limited to man-and-woman rivalry. It can infect any human heart.)

Competition between husband and wife is perhaps the most devastating kind. Its effects can penetrate into the lives of their children and through them to their grandchildren.

Over and over again, my heart goes out to a married woman who faces the problem of "being scripturally subservient" to a man who turned out to be, at best, an inadequate human being! The Apostle Paul does say ". . . a husband is head of his wife, as Christ is Head of His church." This poses a real problem for the woman who discovered after marriage, that her husband is still a child emotionally. This happens, you know. Perhaps it has happened to you.

Men are people, too, and often they don't follow the Biblical ideal set up for them any more than do their wives. Great wisdom is needed here. Constant contact with the God who promises to give wisdom to all who ask!

If a man is emotionally still a little boy, is his wife to follow him into irresponsibility and bad judgment? Here we must remember that Paul also had a word for husbands: "Husbands, love your wives, even as Christ loved the church and *gave Himself* for her." We jump to many eccentric conclusions when we concentrate either on the admonition to the wife or to the husband, forgetting that this passage in Ephesians 5 *begins* with Paul addressing *both* husband and wife: "Be submissive *to one another* out of reverence for Christ."

Paul was a single man, so far as we know, but he spoke with the wisdom of the God who lived in him. Seeing with God's insight, Paul knew the marriage relationship could never work on a competitive basis! He did not say, "Wives, outdo or out-think your husband." He did not say, "Husbands, lord it over your wife." He said they were both to be submissive to each other.

If a woman's husband is immature, and out of that frequently swaggering immaturity, demands that she be his doormat, the Scriptures simply do not back him up! Neither do they back up the wife who expects her husband to carry her around on a pillow. This is not the way Christ treats His church. He *gave Himself* for the church, but He also said, "Follow Me."

The solution to this unfortunate kind of competition between husband and wife is the same as the solution to the same kind of competition which arises often between friends or co-workers. We are to be *submissive* to each other. *This spirit of mutual submission* — mutual consideration for each other — is the only remedy for the problem of unhealthy competition.

"My husband is a darling," one woman said, "but he has never grown up! He just doesn't *want* to be the head of the house." How did this lead to competition between them?

When the husband refused the responsibility of disciplining the children, they turned against their mother, who was stuck with doing it alone. The mother became jealous of their seeming affection for their father, and the rivalry began.

Fair competition in sports, games, business, contests of various kinds, can be a beneficial stimulus. In one sense, "rivalry" can be valuable. But when our emotions become so involved that we cease to be healthy competitors and begin to be ruled by our *competitive spirits,* trouble stalks the scene.

Jesus Christ never put Himself in *competition* with the rulers of this earth. He had to leave His beloved cousin, John the Baptist, in prison because if He had performed a miracle even for faithful John, He would have put Himself in *competition* with Herod. Christ was about the business of establishing a *new kingdom,* unlike anything that had ever existed on earth before. He did not come to prove His superiority, but to give man His Spirit! And His Spirit is always, under all circumstances, the Spirit of love and giving.

"If anyone does not have the Spirit of Christ, he does not belong to Him."

The Spirit of Christ is the Spirit of *understanding cooperation,* not of competition.

10: These Problems
in Relationships

10:

THESE PROBLEMS IN RELATIONSHIPS

In the final chapters we will move into the positive aspects of the problems discussed so far. In the belief, however, that *seeing* the real issues involved is "half the battle," it is now time to summarize some of the disastrous consequences when these particular problems crash into the world of *human relationships.*

Unless the Christian way is workable within the framework of the human family which God created, it is merely a panacea — a personal "spiritual" pillow, as it were, for the comfort of the individual believer. This is not only totally unrealistic, it is impossible. God did create a human family, and all of our individual twists and weaknesses entangle other people. "Each man is an island," but it is most unlikely that anyone reading this book actually lives on an island. We live with people. We work with people. We share a community with people. No amount of longing for the so-called undisturbed bliss of "island living" can change the fact that either God has a way for us to get along with the other people He has put here or He doesn't.

He is not a quixotic God, so of course, He has a way.

In the preceding chapters we have looked at eight problems: *doubt, ingratitude, ignorance, darkness, extremism, conditioning, busyness* and *competition.* These are not all, by any means, but they are all basic. In each of the chapters devoted to each of these problems, are illustrations from everyday life. We will continue and develop that here, both by way of summary and for further insight into some of the real issues behind the frustrations common to so many human relationships.

HUMAN RELATIONSHIPS AND DOUBT

"My mother nags every Sunday for my brother and me to go to Sunday school. You'd think the world would come to an end if we didn't! But she never acts as though she believes God can do anything at all. How does my mother expect us to believe what we hear there, when *she* doesn't after all the years she went to church?"

When this young teen-ager was pressed for an example of her mother's *doubting*, she said: "Oh, she just worries all the time. She worries about whether I will make the honor roll, whether my Dad will make a sale, whether my kid brother will get sick again — all kinds of things. I finally stopped saying my prayers at night because if Mother has to keep on worrying even though she prays all the time, what good is it?"

This girl's mother (quite unconsciously I'm sure) is wrecking the foundation of faith in the lives of both her children, while she goes on nagging them to attend Sunday school. Sunday school teachers are, in the main, noble creatures, who give their time and energies charitably, but they simply cannot be expected to make miracles on a Sunday morning! Not only is this mother's habitual worry pattern wrecking the budding faith of her children in God, the girl's attitude toward her mother plainly shows a deep, growing relationship problem in that home. She, at least, is losing faith, not only in God, but in her mother's sense of values. She sees *through* her mother. The last thing a child should see in a parent is *instability*. Children have a right to have stable parents. James says: "A double-minded person is unstable in all his ways." This mother is double-minded. One part of her nags the children to go to Sunday school in order to learn about the faithfulness of God, and the other part of her mind shows them only *doubt* of this same God.

Young people sense much more than older people give them credit for sensing.

"My wife's a strong Christian," a husband wrote. "She teaches a Bible class and the ladies all think she's tops. So do I! I'm mighty proud of her for doing this, especially when it is hard for her to speak publicly. But why is it she doesn't find out in that Bible she teaches that God can be trusted with *everything?* Bless her heart, I love her so much, but sometimes she nearly drives me to distraction by forcing her anxiety down my throat! I'm a real estate man, and I have to take some risks in my business. I pray every day to do my best and leave the outcome to the Lord. We've been married eighteen years this year, and I don't remember a single deal I've made that hasn't caused some kind of tension between my wife and me. I tried to ignore it for years, thinking it was 'just like a woman' to be anxious. But in the last ten years we've met some other Christian couples and these wives aren't like mine. I honestly don't think I'm an impractical business man. I've made a good living all these years. But lately, I find myself beginning to feel shaky inside. If she doesn't believe in me after all this time, maybe I am a 'gambler,' as she says. The only way I know to keep trouble at a minimum is not to tell her anything at all about the business. I don't want to hide things from her, when I'm not ashamed of anything! But I don't know what else to do."

This woman may need professional help at this late date. But the consequences, at least, are clear. She can teach a Bible class, but she can't trust her own husband to God! Result? Damaged *relationship* in an otherwise successful marriage. Of course, there are many women who do have "gamblers" for husbands. This does not imply that the men are always good in their judgment. But this man has made a good living all their married life, and most likely he has generally sound business judgment.

Why, indeed, can this woman not see from her Bible that it is not her husband, but God whom she doubts? This entire situation could backfire on her one day. If one plants the seed of doubt in another person often enough, it will eventually sprout.

"My father died a year ago, and since then, Mother is such a burden to my sister and me, we are about ready to throw up our hands! I know her heart is broken over his death, and I know she is lonely. But what about the faith she managed to instill in us? Why can't Mother really trust Jesus Christ to heal her grief? She very wisely wants to live alone and says she wants to make her own life. My sister and I do everything for her we know to do, but even visiting her now is such a depressing thing, we both hate the thought of it."

At least they can be thankful that this woman chooses to live her own life. No widow can ever fully recover from her grief, if she puts her children's lives at the center of hers as a substitute. This is false all around. There must be fresh creativity in any healing process, and there can be no creativity when people are forced into unnatural substitute positions. It is perhaps the most difficult adjustment a woman ever has to make, to begin a new life after the death of her life partner, but women do it all the time. And when they are willing to trust Him, they find God is there giving them His full attention and interest in the new project.

When we are afraid of a new thing, we are basically in doubt about God's interest in it with us.

(In Chapter 15 we will deal further with the widow's adjustment to her new life.)

Examine yourself and your personal relationships now. Is your God big enough to handle your situation? And do you trust His judgment enough to expect Him to handle it in the best possible way?

No matter what the dilemma, you *can* "cast your care upon Him," because He *does* care for *you.*

Human Relationships and INGRATITUDE

"I feel like a heel telling you this, but I want so much to do something about it *now*, before it goes on any longer. I love my wife so much, and I don't do anything for her just for purposes of getting her to thank me! I don't care if she ever thanks me for anything. A man is supposed to take care of his wife, and taking care of Janie is the thing I like the very most of all. But now, during the second year of our marriage, when things are kind of settling down after the honeymoon stage, I can see her getting to be more and more like her mother! Don't get me wrong, I get along fine with my mother-in-law, but that woman complains about *everything*. In a crisis, they're both fine! When my father-in-law was seriously ill, both Janie and her mother were real troopers. But it's the little things they grumble about. If I get seats for a concert, they're never good enough. The refreshments at the circle meeting were 'icky.' The new organist at the church can't play like the old one. The new car burns too much gasoline. I'm just plain grateful that I could afford a new car. I think we should be grateful that the new organist will put up with the choir director's disposition. I think it's wonderful that we can buy tickets to a good concert. What a horrible world it would be without music! When I tell Janie these things, she calls me Pollyanna. Frankly, I'm just plain scared. I don't want to have to begin 'putting up' with my wife like some other fellows I know. I *want* to stay really in love with her. It seems to me so much of our fun together is spoiled because she is always complaining. Can she get over this, in spite of the fact that she's heard her own mother do it all her life?"

Ingratitude for the little things, turning into a big, destructive thing. Yes, Janie can get over her habitual complaining *when she sees the danger for herself.* Remember, *seeing* your need in God's presence, puts you on your way to living *through* your problem. The habit of complaining is nothing more than a manifestation of the habit of *ingratitude*.

Many years ago, I lived in an apartment building between two other similar buildings. In the basement apartment of these other buildings, lived two women who were
both real "characters," even though they were direct
opposites. One of these women, in her early sixties, was
named Joy. She couldn't have had a more ridiculous name!
Joy was in excellent health, her son visited her regularly,
kept her well supplied with firewood and good food. Her
basement apartment was well heated and she was well
clothed and fed. She had a television set and a radio and
her son subscribed to all the magazines she could read, even
though he was not well-to-do. But Joy was utterly joyless!
She griped about everything. The same Chicago snow and
ice that inconvenienced us all, somehow singled out Joy for
more discomfort.

I walked my dog past her front door one beautiful
snowy afternoon, as she was shoveling the snow away from
her basement entrance. I didn't have to start a conversation, Joy was already grumbling as she shoveled.

My dog and I hurried on down the block as fast as
possible. All the neighbors dodged getting into a conversation with Joy.

Outside the building on the other side of my apartment,
a frail, stooped little lady in her middle seventies, was also
shoveling the snow away from her depressing little under-
ground apartment. My doggie went wiggling up to her,
happily.

"Good afternoon!" she smiled at us both, stooping to
scratch my dog's head. "Isn't the snow beautiful? They can
say all they want to about our Chicago weather, but when
the snow is fresh and white like this, I think it's glorious!"

This neighbor's name was Sally, and her apartment was
dark and poorly heated. She had no children at all. No
living relatives. She lived on her meager old age pension.
The rest of us who loved her in the neighborhood kept her
supplied with books and took turns keeping her tiny old
radio repaired. The children loved her, the dogs loved her
— even the pre-Beatnik Bohemians loved Sally. Why? Be-

cause she spread *gratitude* around our somewhat dismal city block like a bright blanket of spring sunshine. And she was the only person in the neighborhood who managed to get along with Joy.

Now that I see how ingratitude can breed feelings of inferiority and self-pity, I can look back on these two neighbors and understand why Joy was always running herself down.

"No point in my going to the neighborhood meeting tonight. Who'd pay any attention to me even if I did tell them what's wrong?"

Sally was always at the meetings. Sometimes she talked, sometimes she didn't. But she always made us glad she was there.

"Me complain?" she used to say. "Why, I'm a child of God!"

A grateful heart is truly a "merry heart," and a truly "merry heart (not only) maketh a cheerful countenance" for those with whom it lives, it really does "have a continual feast."

Human Relationships and IGNORANCE

A careful reading of the book of Proverbs will give you a thorough conviction that God is in favor of our acquiring *knowledge.* "The heart of a discerning person *seeks* knowledge." God did not create the human brain for inactivity.

"How long, O simple ones, will you love being simple? How long . . . will fools despise knowledge?"

Academic training and mental brilliance are not required for a man or woman to become a balanced follower of Jesus Christ, but God's Word calls persons who despise knowledge — fools. It is a common thing to hear a certain type of religious person declare that "God must love the common people, because He created so many of them." Abraham Lincoln said this first, so far as I know, but he did not say God loved the common people *best.* God's love is in no way governed by our knowledge or lack of it. God's love is governed only by God's heart. I don't see any scriptural backing for the saying whatsoever. God's Word seems to be brimming with admonitions to us to acquire knowledge.

"The Lord gives wisdom; from His mouth comes knowledge and discernment."

Those among God's children who scoff at learning and the development of one's mind, in reality scoff at God Himself. Cultural taste is not required for admission to the Kingdom of God, but kindness *is*. The Christian, who finds no place in the holy life for what he disdainfully labels "culture," is simply not thinking through the real issues. This does not mean that Christians should gobble up every form of so-called entertainment labeled "cultural." It means just the opposite, in fact. The Christian must *think* through the real issues. We need not take anyone's word for this but God's.

"If any one of you lacks wisdom, let him ask of God, who gives to everyone without reserve and without fault-finding, and it will be granted him."

In other words, God won't find fault with you no matter how confused you are. He will simply set you straight. In no way is it suggested here that all knowledge is profitable. You and I simply have the privilege of going straight to the Lord Himself to find out what knowledge is right for us in our particular circumstance.

"My mother-in-law and I are having it around the barn these days," a young mother wrote. "She thinks I'm being a bad influence on my small children because I read other books to them beside out-and-out Christian literature. I read Bible stories to them, of course. But my mother read *Winnie the Pooh* to me and I'm still delighted with it! I was also brought up in a Christian home, but thank God, it was a *balanced* one."

By the wildest stretch of no one's imagination could there be anything wrong with *Winnie the Pooh!* I try to read it at least once a year and I'm 46. Real *relationship* problems are beginning here between this young mother and her husband's mother because the older woman has a closed mind.

Another woman said, "My husband and I have been having trouble for weeks now, ever since I began taking our son and daughter, aged 7 and 10, to the Art Institute on Saturday afternoons. I want them to be acquainted with the great masterpieces there, and I believe they should be taken. My daughter, particularly, is keenly interested in painting and seems to have real talent. Their father really exploded when he found out where we had been going. He says 'most of that junk isn't fit for the kids to see!' He is a good husband and father, but hates anything that has to do with classical music and art, and feels it will make snobs of the children. My daughter will be heart-broken if we have to stop going."

Rigidity of the kind this man possesses is one of the real danger signals in a human personality. *He* doesn't happen to care for art, so he wants to see to it that his children don't either. Perhaps down inside, he feels inferior for not having developed this side of his mind, perhaps not. At any rate, his *ignorance* is showing itself, not so much in his lack of knowledge about art, but about human nature. He is "playing God" with his little family. He is also being utterly superficial, by judging the big, glorious world of art by his own undeveloped taste. The human relationship problem in his family will grow and grow, unless Dad decides to start doing some growing himself!

In both of these illustrations, there is not only a deplorable lack of practical knowledge of human nature, but an equally deplorable *ignorance* about God Himself. God will give a parent judgment (His judgment) to decide these issues, but in no case will He force His judgment into a locked mind.

When a man or woman is proud of his "ignorance" and scoffs at those who seek after knowledge, he or she is showing an attitude of heart in direct opposition to the heart of Jesus. "I am meek and lowly in heart," He said of Himself. A proud, arrogant, scoffing heart cannot be meek and lowly.

This type of arrogant heart can only cause storms in the area of human relationship.

A mind hungry for knowledge is admirable, but here once more, *humility* is a necessity. We must be humble enough to take God's word for what is right to know and what is wrong. Our first parents started a whole realm of trouble by merely wanting to "know" as much as God knew! Persons with open minds can hear God's word here. If God teaches us something, it is worth knowing. (And remember, God is in the world of art, music and science too. Many people do not know this, but *He* does!)

Christians need to stay very close to His heart, or they can begin acquiring knowledge just for the sake of knowledge. *Knowing* is not enough. *What* we know is the point. God never tries to confuse us. Much of what we get from God seems ridiculous to those who do not know Him, but if we get it from His Word, we can depend upon it.

One can cause plenty of trouble by merely *knowing.* It is quite possible to know a wrong thing and therefore have a trouble-making wrong effect on the group around you.

As in the instance of the healing of Jairus' daughter, according to St. Luke's story:

"On reaching the (Jairus') home, He (Jesus) allowed no one to enter with Him, except Peter, John, and James, and the child's father and mother. Everyone was wailing and beating the breast for her (the child.) But He remarked, 'Stop wailing! She is not dead, but asleep!' And *knowing* that she was dead, they laughed at Him!"

In the presence of the Son of God, these people laughed because they *knew the wrong thing.* They not only laughed, they laughed at God Himself — not knowing who He was! According to their "closed minds" (due to ignorance of Him *and* due to their own conditioning), they *knew* the girl to be dead. Even her parents, who had faith enough to call for Jesus, "were amazed" when He raised her up.

Ignorance of the nature of God is perhaps, the most serious ignorance of all. A mother owes it to her child to give him or her the joy of being able to say at school, "Oh, I already know that painting. My mother showed it to me!"

Parents owe their children exposure to general knowledge. *But a man or a woman with a twisted knowledge of God acquired in childhood, is the most skillful of all troublers of the waters of human relationships.*

"My daughter is a sweet Christian — perhaps too sweet! She has taken up with a woman who is a dreadful alcoholic with the idea of leading her to Christ. This is fine, and I am proud of my daughter, but she keeps wanting to bring this woman to our home. Last week she brought her to dinner, and the woman was so drunk she fell on our top step. I simply can't have this kind of thing going on for the neighbors to see. They know we're Christians and heaven only knows what they think already. What can I do?"

Dear unknowing lady — you can shed your ignorance of the nature of the God who loves this woman as much as He loves you, and be thankful you have not twisted your daughter's idea of Him.

"Grace and peace be yours in abundance *through* intimate acquaintance with God and with Jesus our Lord."

HUMAN RELATIONSHIPS AND DARKNESS

"Perhaps you don't get many letters from non-believers. I do not believe in Jesus Christ as my own Saviour. At least, not yet. I must want to, however, or I wouldn't be disturbed about my neighbor. I have read two of your books, and the God you write about doesn't even seem related to the One my neighbor talks about! Every time we have a party, she is Johnny on the spot at the back fence when I empty the beer cans the next morning. By now, I am convinced that her 'god' is at least a distant relative of Carrie Nation! Isn't there more to the Christian life than that one dare not drink or laugh out loud after midnight?"

Yes, there is. And this awkward human relationship between these neighbors — one, pagan and hungry — the other zealous and in semi-darkness — is an all too common situation.

No one argues that my correspondent is pagan and hungry. Some of you will wonder why I say the other neighbor is in *semi-darkness*. I believe her to be. There is much more to all of life than empty beer cans and post-midnight loud laughter. Neither, however, has anything appreciable to do with a true witness for Jesus Christ which this zealous lady surely intended to be making.

Her Bible states just as clearly as yours and mine, the words of Jesus: "*I*, if *I* be lifted up from the earth, will draw all men unto Me."

He did not say "anti-alcoholism, if anti-alcoholism be lifted up from the earth, will draw all men unto Me." He said "I, if *I* be lifted up."

I am sure this well meaning neighbor has read those glorious words of His, perhaps more times than I have read them. *But* her behavior in this instance, indicates that she is still in *darkness* where their true meaning is concerned.

Much of your darkness in this area can be dispelled if you will read Rosalind Rinker's book, *You Can Witness With Confidence* (Zondervan). I have mentioned it once briefly, but it is with real interest in *your witness*, that I urge you to study it carefully.

There is no place in the realm of human relationship where real revealed light from God is more needed than when you are attempting to witness to your faith in Christ to someone who does not know Him.

Not only does He lead you to the Scriptures which will be helpful to that particular person, but He will lead you to an understanding of the person himself. There is such a vast amount of *knowing* which we cannot grasp with our own intellects, *spiritual* enlightenment becomes absolutely essential when we witness. Otherwise we will do sometimes irreparable damage.

Jesus promised that He would ask the Father to send the Spirit of Truth (God's own Holy Spirit) to reveal to us the things our darkened human minds cannot understand. He always keeps His promises. And this *revealed knowledge* is needed in all human relationships.

I find people who were once difficult for me to understand, now far more understandable, since I had to ask

God's light on my own darkness, in writing my book, *Beloved World.* Here I was telling the story of the Bible. I had to know something about the personalities of the Bible characters. In order to give them lines to speak, I needed to know what motivated their thoughts and actions. The Holy Spirit, through the Scriptures, gave me much needed light. (I can think of no better way to begin to understand someone than to find his or her prototype in the Scriptures and then go to God.)

Last summer, as I was sharing some of the light I had been given on the personality of Jesus' disciple, Thomas, I noticed a young woman in a front seat listening more and more intently. I mentioned that Thomas was born a pessimist; that his mind was *not* an evil mind because he constantly questioned Jesus. He just had to have his individual questions settled for himself, in a way he could understand. He was not nagging the Master, or cooking up doubts, he just wanted to get hold of the facts for himself. After I finished talking, the woman said to me, "Now I can understand my eleven-year-old son!"

God had given her *revealed light.* I was not talking about how to understand one's children. But God knew her need and so He, through His Holy Spirit, dispelled her special darkness. Without doubt, the relationship between this mother and her son will be better from now on. There is *light* on it.

Without doubt we can all find not only the "light of the knowledge of God . . ." but light for the understanding of other people, by the Holy Spirit ". . . in the face of Jesus Christ." Spend more time with Him, discussing the personalities of those with whom you enjoy or endure human relationships. He will help you to understand them.

Human Relationships and EXTREMISM

"My teen-aged son is so extreme in everything he does! If he makes a new boy-friend, he wants to be with that boy all the time. If their interest is guns (as it is at the moment),

I pick up gun magazines, target pistols, even shotguns from my living room floor constantly it seems. Bob is my only son, and since I don't have other children to compare him with, I wonder if this is normal."

Yes, it is — for a teen-ager! *Extremism* is one of the most flagrant characteristics of the teens. They are extreme and fickle. Every recording favorite of this age group knows he had better make hay while the time is right. Next year, or next month, his teen fans may be swooning over someone else. One thing is certain, they will always be *extremely* interested somewhere about someone or something. *Extremism* is normal for the teen-ager.

Serious trouble results from it, however, when this immature tendency to extremes is carried over to the middle twenties and beyond.

"My wife wants to do nothing but go to church, church, church. I'm a Christian and I love our church, too. But now and then I enjoy a concert or a ball game, but she will never go along with me. What does a man do when his wife *churches* him half to death?"

He prays for her to grow up! The church was never intended to occupy the whole of the human life. It is a place where those who belong to Jesus Christ, meet to worship Him and to communicate His love to those who do not know Him. Persons who really *belong* to Christ, have caught some of His balance. Because one tends to be extreme toward a *good* thing, like the church, or reading, or even generosity, does not lessen the trouble that can result. The point is to learn how to redistribute our energies and interests so that we are not extreme in anything.

This, of course, is the ideal goal. It cannot be accomplished over night, and it can never be accomplished by human effort alone. The last fruit of the Spirit, according to Paul's letter to the church at Galatia, is *self-control* (temperance) — the state of not tipping too far one way or another in anything. "There is no law against these" (fruits of the Spirit). In other words, no one gets into trouble with any law — moral, spiritual, traffic or federal — by being *balanced*.

True, a balanced Christian can experience trouble when his balanced nature is confronted with the imbalance of an *extremist*. The man whose wife is "churching him half to death" knows this. Any wife whose husband never knows when to stop watching TV at night knows it, too. The daughter who is forced to live with her self-pitying widowed mother knows it. But these balanced individuals are in truth sharing the sufferings of Christ Himself. His holy, balanced nature crashed into the sinful *extremism* of man at Calvary.

When a man or woman truly begins to allow God to make him or her a balanced individual, this in no way means that troubled days are over for that person. It does mean, however, that he or she is not adding to the world's confusion any longer. The truly redemptive life has begun. Identification with Christ Himself becomes a reality to that person. His human life is *justified*. He is a contributor, not a destroyer.

Alcoholics are invariably extremists. They cannot stop with one or two drinks.

Gossips are invariably extremists. They cannot stop with telling only the necessary parts of a story.

Overweight people are extremists. They cannot stop with the amount of food adequate to supply their nutritional needs.

Spendthrifts are extremists. They cannot stop spending within the bounds of their income.

Pennypinchers are extremists. They cannot stop loving their money more than they love people in need.

Flatterers are extremists. They cannot stop talking until they have seen some *self-elevating* effect of their words.

Critical people are extremists. They cannot stop plying their own opinion long enough to feel the possible pain in the hearts of the people they condemn.

The list is long and ugly.

Extremists cannot be glad unless their extremes are being satisfied. Paul wrote: "Be glad in the *Lord* always;

again I say, Be glad! Be known by all the people for your *considerateness;* the Lord is near."

Extremists are never considerate people.

Are you considerate, not only by your standards of consideration, but by the standards of the other person? By the standards of Christ Himself?

Are you jumpy with fear? Does this make you inconsiderate of other people because your fear is so extreme you just have to prove your point or have your own nerves settled — even if it is at the expense of someone else? Normal fear is healthy. If you did not fear electricity, you would never have that broken outlet fixed. But *extreme* fear is not only unhealthy, it creates havoc around you.

"The Lord is near" to change your fear to courage.

Fearful people are extremists, but Jesus says, "Be not afraid, it is I."

Anxious people are extremists, but Jesus says, "Have no care for tomorrow."

Worried people are extremists, but the Word of God says, "Entertain no worry, but under all circumstances let your petitions be made known before God. . . ."

We cannot let go of our troublesome extremes alone, but "the Lord is near" to help us.

"Let that mind which was in Christ Jesus be in you."

HUMAN RELATIONSHIPS AND CONDITIONING

My mother vows that when I was a tiny baby, I cried very little. I was her first-born, so perhaps she was enjoying the immunity of young mothers to any jarring feature concerning the first baby. At any rate, she does remember one lusty few moments of chaos I created while lying in my crib in the kitchen where she was preparing dinner one stormy evening during my first summer on earth. A gigantic crack of thunder startled me into making up for all the noise I hadn't been making. Of course, she dropped her dinner preparations and rushed to me. It seems I reacted in the same panic every time the thunders rolled for several months. Naturally, I remember none of that. What I do remember clearly, at about the age of three, is sitting on Mother's lap, her left arm securely around me, while she pointed with her right hand toward the herculean clouds rolling across another stormy summer sky. We laughed together at the thunder and imagined we saw horses and castles with turrets in the cloud patterns, and I even "found" a little girl there, with a wide, starched skirt, and carrying a basket of flowers on her arm! Storms had definitely and permanently lost their terror for me. I love them now.

What was happening to me there on Mother's lap, "finding things" in the sky? I was being *conditioned* to love.

One of the things I liked best as a child, was for my handsome father to carry me while we took long tramps through the woods near our summer cottage. His arm was so strong and his shoulder so wide and ample, and I "rode" so high in the air, I could pull off sassafras leaves from trees I could never have reached had I been down on the ground walking along on my own feet.

My favorite place to be carried was on the back of Dad's neck, with one short, stubby leg over each of his big shoulders. When my brother Joe came along, three years after I did, Dad had quite a problem, but his muscles were strong and I reconciled myself to being carried on one big forearm again, while my roly-poly little brother bounced along on the other forearm. I still have a snapshot of Dad carrying us both like that. It is one of my dearest possessions. The expression on my face, even squinting against the sunlight, is one of utter happiness. Riding up there in the heights in the big arms I loved so much, I was all gladness. I was on my Daddy's arm and all was well with the world.

Once more, I was being *conditioned* to love.

When at last I discovered the identity of God in Jesus Christ, I believed at once that He loved me. I had been wonderfully *conditioned* by both my parents to accept love freely. When parents condition their children to love, they are conditioning them to God, because "God is love."

You may not be actually teaching your child Bible verses every moment, but if you are showing that child love, you are preparing his heart for God Himself.

Children don't always understand all the teaching they receive, but they do understand the language of love. If their hearts have been conditioned to receive and return love, they will always be able to do it.

Conditioning in itself is neither good nor bad. As we mentioned in Chapter 7, we are all conditioned. It is the kind and extent of the conditioning that counts.

"I have been taught since childhood to doubt the salvation of anyone who wears make-up, particularly lipstick," one woman wrote. "This has caused me trouble all my life. I do not wear it, but I just have to believe *you* are a true Christian, and I know you wear it because you said so in your book, *Woman to Woman*. Please tell me how I can get out of the habit of thinking this way. My head tells me better, but I still shy away from women with lipstick, wondering if they are saved or not."

When this woman's child mind was open and receptive, she could just as easily have been taught to look for the signs of humility, kindness and patience in the Christian woman. *Conditioning* need not always be negative!

If a child is taught to be suspicious of other people, whether it be their honesty, their religious beliefs, or their political affiliation, that child is being taught a wrong concept of God Himself. If the parent is constantly policing the world in the child's presence, that child will grow up with the idea that God is also a policeman, someone with a big stick, who sees to it that His creatures do not break His law.

This is as far removed from the heart of love and caring which God revealed in Jesus Christ as any concept could possibly be. God is our Father, and the child who plays and works and studies and sleeps, confident of the love of his parents, will know how to accept the true love of the Heavenly Father. Could God be less loving than a loving human parent?

I was overjoyed just last night, as I read the opening chapters of Catherine Marshall's book, *Beyond Our Selves* (McGraw Hill), to find her heart also aching to let the world know the extent of the love of our Father for His loved ones. I titled my own recent book *Beloved World* from my deepening conviction that we can't imagine on this earth, the height and depth and breadth of the love of God for every member of His "beloved world."

If your own early *conditioning* has been negative, this God we follow is powerful enough to break it up and *recondition* you in the Love of the giving heart that broke on Calvary. If your *conditioning* has been the conditioning of love, give thanks, and pass it along. The world needs to know about love, more than it needs anything else. And love *cannot* be legislated.

HUMAN RELATIONSHIPS AND BUSYNESS

I'm sure I could not tell you how she did it, but in spite of housework, cooking, and a heavy load of church activities (including directing the church choirs), my mother managed to take a nap with my brother and me almost every day when we were children.

She didn't just send us off to bed, she went, too. And it was always a real "production." We didn't merely sleep. I suppose we did that, too, but I have riotous memories of making tents out of Mother's good sheets, of vigorous pillow fights (she had special old pillows we brought out for this) and of loud vocalizing in what must have been a fearful sounding, but energetic trio of voices, Mother's, Joe's and mine. We made up stories about long, exciting river expeditions and always we acted them out. Our home was on a big river, and in those days, the famous old river boats, the "Gordon C." and the "Chris Green," still raced each other past our house. I was always the "Gordon C." and Joe the "Chris," and we wiggled on our stomachs "racing" up and down the bed, tooting our whistles and churning the linen. Mother was the crowd "cheering" from the river bank.

Somehow she managed her busy, busy schedule, so that my brother and I never felt left out of her life. In fact, so far as we knew, we *were* her life. My Dad always found time to hunt and fish with my brother, to play baseball with us both and we seldom missed a Twilight League game in the summer.

When Joe and I had a "project" going, which we usually had, one of our parents always managed time to be on hand. My first "immortal" lines were written in the plays I dashed off and directed. My cast was all star and versatile. It consisted of my pudgy kid brother, the red-haired Scottish boy whose family lived in my grandmother's apartment building next door, and me. Dad bought the lumber we needed for stage building, paid a regular one dollar admission charge (or more if we were short), drank quarts of 10¢ lemonade made from lemons he had bought for us, and faithfully sat through every performance, an audience of one — reading his newspaper. We didn't mind that he didn't watch. He was there, and that's what mattered. My father was a busy professional man, with many outside business activities, too.

I have friends now, who also make time to be with their children. I realize that I speak from territory foreign to me, since I don't have this problem myself. But apparently it is possible for parents to spend enough time with their children, so the youngsters feel at home with them.

God needs us to be with Him too. Of course, no one is ever out of the Presence of God. "Lo, I am with you always." But most of us seldom remember this. We go madly about dashing carelessly in and out of the *consciousness* of His presence, and almost every person who prays asks God "to be with us." This is not only an unfortunate habit in prayer, it shows us up as we really are — not always at home with Him!

How long has it been since you have really sat quietly in the Lord's presence and read slowly and thoughtfully the beautiful poetry of David's 23rd Psalm?

Here it is now, for us both, in the dear familiar words of the King James Bible:

> The Lord is my *shepherd;* I shall not want, He maketh me to *lie down* in green pastures; he leadeth me beside the *still waters.* He *restoreth* my soul; he leadeth me in the paths of righteousness for his name's sake. Yea, though I walk through the valley of the shadow of death, I will fear no evil, for *thou art with me;* thy rod and thy staff they *comfort me.* Thou preparest a table before me in the presence of mine enemies: *thou* anointest *my* head with oil; *my cup runneth over.* Surely *goodness* and *mercy* shall *follow me* all the days of my life: and I will dwell in the house of the Lord forever.

The italics are mine. A shepherd is a quiet man, intent only on caring for his sheep. This Lord is our *shepherd.* He wants to quiet us, to make us "to lie down" and realize His presence. If we are following Him, we will be where the waters are still. The drinking will be good. Our feverish panting will be eased. We will not be anxious or worried for the simple, child-like reason that *He is with us.* This great God longs to anoint our heads. Even He cannot do this if we are always putting our hats on to go still another place! If we stop long enough to remember Him, our cups *will* run over, because of what He is like. And wonder of wonders, He is *following* us — even at our breakneck speeds — with both His goodness and His mercy!

The Lord who is already your shepherd, is waiting now for you to check your schedule *with Him.* He will guide you if your efforts to curtail your *busyness* are sincere.

Human Relationships and COMPETITION

Competition, without a doubt, is one of the most easily tripped over problems. And yet, it is a virulent resentment breeder.

We *resent* our rivals. The *competitive* heart soon comes to resent its competitor, if Christ is not completely in control.

The man who does not prosper in his business, soon resents his competitors and God. That is, he resents God if he is still living in the Old Testament. There is nothing in the Gospel of Jesus Christ which promises a man prosperity in exchange for a pious life.

When I was collecting material for my book, *Woman to Woman,* I asked a provocative question of hundreds of teen-agers: "What's wrong with your mother?" The answer I got with startling frequency went something like this: "She is always comparing me with some other kid!"

One freckled-faced girl wrinkled up her little nose and snapped, "Yeah, 'why can't you be a nice, quiet girl like cousin Phyllis'? I see red when my mother says this!"

Cousin Phyllis immediately became this girl's rival.

Remember, the dictionary defines *competition* as "a contest between rivals." Contests are fine, but people should not be put into competition with each other in the business of living.

A deeply distressed woman once said to me: "My husband has a strange streak in him where our children are concerned. It almost seems to me like he is my rival. He seems always to be trying to influence our son and daughter over to his side, away from me."

A minister's wife — a thoroughly capable, intelligent woman — has put her somewhat weaker minded husband in painful competition with the members of his church board. She feels (and perhaps rightly so) that these men are holding her husband back in his efforts to expand their church. There seems to be much to back up this woman's thinking, but there is nothing to back up her attitude of heart. One of the ladies of the church overheard this minister's wife give him his send-off from the parsonage back porch on his way to a board meeting. She patted him on the shoulder briskly, and said, "Now, go get 'em, honey! Don't let anyone get the best of you!"

On the surface this sounds like good, laudable wifely interest and encouragement. But because of the attitude of her heart — obviously filling up with resentment against the men with whom her husband must work—she is creating chaos.

Are you creating chaos somewhere by consciously or unconsciously putting your husband, your friends, your child, yourself, in competition with someone? Is resentment building because of it? Is it being divisive and creating discord? Then, think "how good and how pleasant it is for brothers (all people) to live harmoniously together! It is like the precious oil upon the head, flowing down..." to spread its fragrance among those whose lives your life touches.

From prison, dear Paul wrote pleadingly to the Christians in the church at Ephesus, "..conduct yourselves worthy of the calling you have received; with unalloyed humility and gentleness in a loving way patiently to bear with one another, making every effort to preserve the *unity* of the Spirit by the binding power of peace..."

The same Paul wrote that "He (Jesus Christ) *is* our peace."

He is there to give you access to His binding power.

In none of these problems has there been specifically a moral issue involved. These are not problems resulting necessarily from obviously "sinful type" behavior. We have considered no shocking thefts of funds and no adulterous flings. The kind of confusion we have been considering is even more insidious because it seems so "normal," so commonplace.

If there is a particular human relationship which is causing you trouble now, take time to think through the real issues. Examine your own part in it, your own attitude. Does your problem of *doubt, ingratitude,* or *lack of knowledge* or *revealed light* create part of the difficulty? Is one of your *extremes* harming someone? Does your early religious *conditioning* or your *busyness* enter into the situation? Or could it be that quite unconsciously you have allowed the *competitive* spirit to invade your heart?

God is eternally interested, and He is right there to begin redeeming the whole situation. After all, He already knows everything about it. Perhaps He has just been waiting for you to begin to think it through in His presence.

11: Understanding Ourselves

II: Understanding Ourselves

11:

UNDERSTANDING OURSELVES

Too many people all over the world of human nature have one sad trait in common: *lack of self-knowledge.* If a woman does not understand herself, how can she possibly understand her husband, her children, her friends? Actually, she blocks their understanding of her because in her own lack of self-knowledge, she presents to them a false "personality."

Our own spoken estimates of ourselves are more revealing than we might like to believe. For example, if you constantly say, "Oh, I don't care," this probably means you *do* care so desperately, your normal caring has in reality turned to *anxiety*. You just can't help talking about it. The truth about you is, however, probably not realized by your family and friends because they have trouble being objective about you. Their emotions are blocking their insight where you are concerned. So, you keep on saying, "Oh, I don't care," and they act toward you as though you're telling the truth. They are careless toward you, and you (because you *do* care desperately) resent it! Somewhere along the line of your life, you have adopted someone else's idea of you. Perhaps your parents labeled you careless. Perhaps so many difficult things have happened to you that you have adopted this "I don't care" attitude as a cover up. Whatever the reason, it is not your real self. It is no one's real self. Everyone cares.

The balanced woman who knows herself doesn't waste time and energy on self-comment. With her own short-comings and attributes well in hand, she goes on about the business of living. She is not complacent, she is simply free. She is on good terms with herself emotionally, and she makes it simpler for other people to remain on good terms with her, too.

If you are one of those persons who goes about in constant self-reference, "I'm just the stubborn type"; or "If there's anything I hate, it's a lie"; or "I'm not the type to mince words! I come right out with it," etc. etc. there is most likely something you're covering up in you from *yourself*. If you talk constantly of how busy you are, could it be that you're covering up guilt for having neglected so many things?

In their readable book, *The Mind Alive* (Norton), Harry and Bonaro Overstreet write: "That a discrepancy often thus exists between self-description and fact has always been recognized. But in our time, something new has been added to this common folk recognition. This 'something new' is the testimony of psychotherapists to the effect that a false estimation of the self — one that demands too much or too little of the individual, or too little of the world in the way of response — is a customary factor in emotional disturbance."

The woman who has a false idea of herself almost inevitably will demand too much or too little of her friends and family. If you do not recognize your own tendency to pity yourself and travel with the mistaken notion that no one does enough for you, you automatically put unreal demands upon your family and friends. True, your life may be hard, but can your close associates really help it? Wouldn't it lighten everyone's load if you stopped to discover *yourself* in the bright, unshadowed light of God's knowledge of you? If you are a believer in Jesus Christ, your journey to self-discovery can be greatly shortened. Within you lives the Holy Spirit of Christ Himself, and He wants to "light you up" so that *you* can see you as you really are.

One woman wrote, "I am beginning to see myself and it is pretty hard to take. Suddenly, I am realizing that I am hogging the conversation, no matter who tries to talk with me. My self-reference is constant. Could it be because I am really so sure I'm *not* important that I talk about myself all the time?"

This woman is a new Christian, and already she is seeing herself as she is. Her next letter shows she is also taking God's grace to accept herself.

"I see now that I talk about myself so much because I am afraid no one will notice me. Also I don't care enough about other people's lives to listen to them talk."

A middle-aged mother told me that she and the Lord were in the process of taking a good, long, realistic look at her.

"I see that I have caused my husband and my children hardship because I was blind to the fact that I slaved at my household chores *expecting* thanks from them, and that I resented it when I didn't get it. After all, that is my work. Why should they (her children) thank me any more than they thank their father for going to the office every day?"

Another mother confessed the wrong she had done her daughter. "All my life I wanted to be a missionary. It didn't work out for me, but I was determined that my daughter should be one. She has just had a nervous break-down on the mission field because she was not being true to herself. God hadn't called her apparently. It was not what *she* should have done. I, her mother, pushed her into it. God help me to forgive myself! I will always hear the dear child weeping from her hospital bed because she was still afraid not to go through with it for fear of hurting me. If I had only seen myself as forcing my own frustrated ambition on my daughter. I brought her up under such stress in her anxiety to please me that she had no chance to find out her real desires and aims. With God's help, we will try to be true to ourselves from now on. My husband sees this, too."

What a different world it would be if only the Christians who live in it would really be true to themselves! But, just as no one can be true to God, unless he or she knows God and knows what He really wants, so no one can be true to oneself without *self-knowledge*.

If you do not know and understand your abilities and limitations and quirks, you simply cannot be fair and realistic in your judgment and treatment of other people. If you do not know your own real motives, you will, many times without realizing it, use other people to further your own image of yourself.

"My mother has come to live with us," writes a minister's wife. "She has made herself a self-styled parish worker, and has taken over the running of the parsonage! When my husband and I don't praise her for her efforts, she reads us the riot act — sometimes right out of the Scriptures, and accuses us of needing to be born again!"

This mother has such an exalted image of her own "spirituality," she is creating havoc in that household because no one else agrees with her image of herself.

"Not only has my mother taken over our home, she has collected around her a little group of adoring women in my husband's church, and she flatters them until they all think she is right and my husband and I are dead wrong on most issues. I know Mother does not realize this. She is a good woman and loves the Lord, but the parsonage and soon the church, are going to be civil war battle grounds."

Perhaps you are not demanding too much of other people, but are expecting too much of *yourself*. This can be just as confusing.

The woman who takes on more than any woman can be expected to do efficiently, is being totally unrealistic about herself and displaying a pathetic lack of self-understanding.

"I am out of things entirely now and flat on my back in bed with a complete physical and nervous collapse. What my family will do, I can't tell you. My girls cannot even iron a shirt! They can open cans or the family would starve, I guess. I lie here hour after hour weeping my eyes out with worry over what will happen to my family without me."

Somewhere along the line, this woman got the idea that in order to be the kind of mother she expected herself to be, she must bend every effort to become indispensable to her family. She did everything! Everything except teach them self-reliance. They were falling apart at the family-seams without her. She has crippled them hopelessly.

"All I have ever wanted," the poor deluded woman moaned in her letter, "was to be physically able to slave and care for my loved ones."

This may sound cruel, but what she really wanted was for her family to depend on her *entirely*, for reasons of her own inflated ego.

A minister, whom I once visited in a hospital, had it straight: "I just tried to do too much. The Lord has now taught me here in this hospital bed, that He is God — I'm not. When I get out of here, I am going to be true to myself. I resisted my congregation when they wanted to get an assistant minister. I see now that it was my exalted image of myself."

Perhaps it would be well right here for us to be clear about the word *ego*. It is not necessarily a bad thing. Unfortunately we glibly label any awkward manifestation of self-centeredness as "ego." The *ego* is simply the *self*. Jesus told us that we are to love our neighbors as much as we love *ourselves*. This certainly does not imply that He felt we were to despise ourselves. We will look more closely at this concept of Jesus' in the next chapter, on *Understanding Self-love*. For now, let it be clear that the *self* is not necessarily to be frowned upon and extinguished! In fact, if you extinguish your *self*, you extinguish *you*. The *ego*, as God originally intended it, is a glorious thing. We were created in God's image. The human *ego* was created after the image of God Himself. Then sin entered the human race and man's ego no longer resembled God's. What we must remember is that no matter how sinful man has become, no matter how twisted his ego, in itself, ego is necessary. It must be if we are to be. There is, in other words, no living without it. Therefore, each human being under God is thoroughly responsible to look at his own *ego* (self) realistically and then take it before God for repairs and redemption.

We are not being unrealistic enough to advise "killing self." Jesus came to redeem your self, so why minimize His efforts by attempting to do away with something He considered so valuable?

You and I need to know ourselves as completely as possible. The prodigal son had to "come to himself," recognize his need, before anything could be done for him, even by such a loving father as the boy had. We must do the same.

How do we get to know ourselves?

First, of all, if you are not already convinced of your need for self-knowledge, take note of what God's Word has to say about people who have one mind for this and another for that: "A double-minded man is *unstable* in all his ways." This is also true of a double-minded woman. If you have one set of standards for yourself and another for your friends, or if you rule your family roost with an eye to your own false image of yourself, you are bound to be unstable. In fact, I believe this potent statement from the Scripture has still a deeper dimension: An *unstable* person is always a double-minded person! It is your lack of reality in your own concept of yourself which causes the instability.

The second step, after we have permitted God to convince us of our need (through an honest look at the circumstances in which we are entangled), is to determine once and for all that *you will be honest about yourself and your needs*. A good way to get the required perspective on yourself is to find a friend who will spend some time helping you. Tell this friend of your sense of need to readjust your *self* to your surroundings. If you are a wife, try to get your husband to be that friend! I once read of a "game" which served this purpose marvelously, particularly for those who live in the same house together. Each person involved writes down two good things about each other person. Then he writes down one bad thing which he would like to see changed. For example, one wife wrote: "I love you, dear husband, for taking such good care of our material needs, and I like the way you carry your Christianity into your business. I do not like the way you interrupt me before guests when I am trying to tell a story."

Anyone will take one criticism in exchange for two compliments.

If no other human being is available for such a time of searching, God is always ready. We can always stand face to face with Jesus Christ and begin to see ourselves as we really are. It is a shocking and disrupting experience in part, but where He is, there is always *hope* and *promise*, because He believes utterly in what we can become *in Him*. His presence has the power of bringing out both the worst and the best in us. His knowledge of us is totally accurate. It is never better than the truth and it is never worse than the truth. It is *realistic* always. When we see our shortcomings in His presence, we need not despair, because *He is a redeemer*. He did not stop being a redeemer when He finished with Calvary. He is still hard at it for us. When we see our good points, in His presence, we are not tempted to pride, but rather, humility and gratitude.

The third step is to realize that sincerity with oneself means that we must recognize what we *can* do as well as what we *cannot* do. It has been said that we must not put our limitations closer to ourselves than God puts them! God wants us to face facts. It is not conceit to recognize one's own abilities. When we cringe and run ourselves down, we are belittling the God who created us. We also belittle Him when we compare ourselves with other people. He made you as you are, with your talents and your limitations.

"After I heard *her* sing," one soprano pouted, "I vowed I'd never sing another solo in church as long as I lived!"

God asks only of you that you be the best "you" possible.

God asks only this of me, of every member of His human family.

The fourth step is to check your *motives* for sincerity. You may be "sincerely" wanting that office in your particular society. But what are your *motives* for wanting it? Don't lie to yourself! This is a grave injustice. We hate other people lying about us, and yet we don't hesitate to lie to ourselves. You are one of God's loved ones and you displease Him deeply when you lie about yourself or to yourself. He feels just as strongly about your being truthful with and about yourself as He feels about your truthfulness in relation to His other loved ones. We all matter terribly to God.

The Christian woman who has come to see and understand herself is more than half-way down the road to the adjustment of her problems. If, however, you have just now made an honest appraisal of yourself, have faced your inferiority feelings, your guilt feelings, your tendency to be overly shy or overly forward and so on, and still feel "unfinished," try this: Take time to remember with the help of the Holy Spirit (whom Jesus said would "Bring all things to our knowledge"), the times God has given you some direct word which you either disobeyed or put aside for further consideration. We all have had times like this. Gradually, a sort of callus grows over the area He longed to change. Eventually we may even forget the thing entirely. These unresolved dealings with God can cloud a woman's knowledge of herself, because in those areas she is living with a self-image she was forced to build. In other words, when God said "Do this," and you did the other thing, you were "forced" to alter your character right there, in order to compensate.

Here is an example from another letter: "I was almost a hundred pounds overweight and I chain smoked when I was converted four years ago. God told me to stop both kinds of gluttony. I stopped smoking, but kept on stowing away the cream puffs and hot chocolate! Result — I began to be terribly critical. Especially of women with nice figures. Now, several stacks of mashed potatoes and many dozen dough-nuts later, I have finally faced up to *me*. I became so critical of my Sunday school teacher who took off forty pounds, I mounted a spiritual pedestal and demanded that

I, too, be made a Sunday school teacher. They were short of hands, of course, so I got a class of ten-year-olds. This was when I faced myself. One little smart-aleck (as I called her inwardly then!) said: 'Miss ——, how come you're so fat when the Bible says we are not to be gluttons?' That did it. I had so covered up my own disobedience to Him where my weight was concerned with my new role of critic, I had almost conveniently forgotten what He had asked me to do! I am now only about fifty-five pounds overweight and determinedly on my way *down* with the Lord! Oh yes, and I asked my svelte Sunday school teacher to take me back in her class. I saw I needed to be *taught*."

When we dare to look at ourselves as we are, in the presence of Christ, good things have to happen; *if* we are willing to *act* on what we see. Catching a glimpse of ourselves as we look to Him, humbles us, but it does not drag us down. It is as though He says, "Yes, that's pretty bad, but come on and walk with Me — *My* way. You'll be surprised at the places you and I can go together."

However ineffectual and unimportant and useless you may feel, you are terribly important to God, and He needs you to be your *best self* so that the part of His great plan which concerns you, can be carried to its glorious completion. In order to be your best self, you must begin now to understand yourself, and He longs to help you.

Part Two

To Peace

12: Understanding Self-love

12:

UNDERSTANDING SELF-LOVE

Among Christians, the expression *self-love* has unfortunately come to mean something to be avoided at any cost. This is far from a true concept.

After all, Jesus said we were to love our neighbor in the same way in which we love ourselves. If He had meant we were not to love ourselves, He would never have used this analogy. On the other hand, He also said we were to deny ourselves. Is this a contradiction? If we face the real issues involved in the concept of love as Jesus taught and demonstrated it, no.

Undoubtedly we are to deny or refuse the kind of destructive self-love which propels us into the same kind of *grabbing* behavior in which Mother Eve indulged herself; but there is a *right* and *creative* kind of self-love which is affirmed by Jesus' instruction to love our neighbors with the same kind of concern which we hold for ourselves. Perhaps *concern* is the key word here to opening this somewhat puzzling concept of self-love. You and I must have genuine, God-directed *concern* for ourselves. If you drink all the coffee you want, just because you want it, this can be destructive. There is no concern here for your real self. There is only a desire gratified for the moment your nerves are screaming for more caffein. If you really care about yourself you will drink only a cup or two and let it go.

As I understand the statement of Jesus relative to loving oneself, there is nothing destructive in real self-love. In fact, if we do not love ourselves, we belittle the God who cared enough about us to create us in the first place. More than that, we hamper our own growth. Here we must make a definite distinction between *hampering* and *pampering*.

The right kind of self-love never *hampers*, but the wrong kind of self-love always *pampers*.

I have just returned from a short but exhausting speaking engagement. The first two days I was home, I slept as long as I wanted to in the mornings. This was not *pampering*. Had I forced myself to get up and go on with this chapter before I was properly rested, I would have been *hampering*. These last chapters are all important. If they are not expressed with clarity, the purpose of the whole book will suffer. However, if I had slept as long as I wanted to this morning, I would have been *pampering* myself. My knowledge of myself and my limitations when I have not had enough sleep, clears the issue here. Some people seem able to go on working day after day, with night after night of short sleep. I cannot. This I know and accept about myself, and act accordingly.

My *motive* here is the key. As far as I know, I did not "sleep in" those mornings just because I enjoyed it. I did enjoy it, but I slept because I knew I would work better after some rest. I have learned to expect very little of myself when I am overly tired. Therefore, when I become irritated or work unevenly, and know that lack of sleep is the cause, I simply go on without discouragement or self-annoyance until I have had a chance to catch up. I do not mean my disposition gives me no concern when I'm tired. I just do not prolong the disturbance or add to it by feeling false guilt. A sense of humor comes gladly to our rescue here. When I'm cross from weariness, I remind those around me of this fact, and ask forgiveness. Then, when I'm rested, I don't have an alibi left.

Too much to eat at bed-time, lack of sleep and adequate

exercise, irregular functional habits, a sagging mattress, or incorrect glasses can cloud the windows of our souls. To mistreat our bodies means we do not love ourselves in the right way.

"I am a Christian," a young man said, "but I must love myself more than I love God or anyone else, because I can't seem to pass my favorite bar on pay-day!"

This boy is dead wrong. He hates himself. He is mistreating himself. Not only by excessive drinking, but because all week long, until the next pay-day, he has loaded himself with anxiety over unpaid bills and guilt over his weakness.

"I guess I just love myself to pieces!" The woman who spoke was waddling along beside me at a summer retreat. She weighed at least two hundred and twenty-five pounds and had been a "fundamental" Christian for thirty years. "When I see a plateful of gravy and mashed potatoes or a big yummy serving of ice-cream, I lose all control. I just shovel it in!"

I still have some weight to lose, but as I walked along beside that woman, my heart ached for her. It was a hot day, and she was dripping and puffing. "I guess I just love myself to pieces," she had said. Not at all. She had no real love or respect for herself. In her central being, she was just like the young man who couldn't pass his favorite bar on pay-day. Both were cruelly mistreating themselves. The wrong kind of self-love is in reality, self-hatred.

Self-indulgence is not the only kind of self-hate or wrong self-love. Here is an example which is much more difficult to apprehend.

"My parents slaved and scrimped to put me through college. I am a school teacher and I despise it! For six years I have strained every effort to adjust to my profession. I try with every ounce of energy to love the children and to have a real interest in them. At the end of every day of these six years, I have hated myself for failing miserably. I feel so ungrateful toward my parents and so ashamed before my students. I just don't understand myself at all."

She certainly did not understand herself. Six years is long enough to try anything for "inner size." This woman finally began to respect herself enough to face the real issues. A good teacher is a *called* one. She re-examined her abilities, applied for a position in personnel work and is now making a good adjustment.

This does not mean that in all cases, restlessness with one's work requires a change. But it does mean that we owe it to ourselves to find out about us, so that we are not forcing our efforts and distorted personalities on other people unnecessarily.

"I hate housework! I hate being tied to the responsibility of three meals a day and four children. In fact, I dodge my responsibilities every chance I get. I got into this mess when I was too young to know my own mind and now I know I should have been a writer. I almost hate *you*, because you're not in prison as I am and can write for a living!"

The school teacher could change jobs. What about this woman? Should she divorce her husband and desert her children? Obviously not. The key lies in the different *tone* of the two letters. The school teacher felt a failure. Her attitude was one of wanting to make a "go" of a wrong choice. The woman who hates her domestic life seems only resentful and sorry for herself. Many women find themselves in this "prison." Many find themselves in the wrong job, as did the school teacher. But the key to *living through* the problem lies, I believe, in first taking stock of our true feelings concerning ourselves. Utmost honesty is required. If we feel simply mistreated and a victim of circumstances, as this housewife so obviously feels, we cannot do more than endure.

Understanding and loving ourselves does not imply the right to self-pity and resentment. Can you imagine Jesus urging us to love ourselves in that destructive way? This housewife's perspective is clouded with self-concern. The school teacher's perspective was clear. She recognized her own short-comings and did something about it. In her case, there was no shirking of her duties, no complaints about her wrong choice of profession. She was honestly asking for help in living through the problem to a creative solution.

The housewife is storing up so much resentment and self-concern, she hates all professional writers who are not tied to domestic duties.

This woman — any woman — can only learn to love herself *in God*. It is not mere theory when we say that God *will* give this distressed housewife His love for her children. Most likely she thinks she does love them now. I doubt it. She is sentimentally attached to them because she gave them birth and regular baths through the years. But if she really loved them, she would not be nurturing her self-pity. My heart goes out to her in real identification. I happen to love my life — all of it. But there are thousands of single women who would change places in a minute with this distraught mother of four children! *Where* we are is not the point. The point is *what* we know ourselves to be. How much respect do we have for our real selves? How well do we know our real selves? And how *free* are we to love ourselves once we have discovered us?

There is a right kind of self-love, and there is a wrong kind.

It seems equally difficult to discover the truth about both. Most of us have both, and then there comes the problem of distinguishing. Which is to be dealt with? Which is to be cultivated?

"I have a friend," one lady confided, "who forces me to spend time with her in order to keep peace! She insists that she loves me so much she will fight for my friendship to the death. If I don't call her every day and have dinner with her at least three times a week, she bombards me with letters and phone calls. She throws scenes and accuses me of being un-Christian. Sometimes I find myself wishing she'd drop dead! Then I am ashamed and guilty. If she loves me this much, why don't I feel more than a sort of dogged dread and pity for her?"

The reason is obvious. This "friend" loves *herself* in the self-centered, destructive way. She does not love the woman who confided in me. She loves the way this woman makes her *feel*. This is totally self-directed love. It is a chain on the heart and mind of the other person involved. When we find our "love" causing strain of any kind for the other person, we can know at once that it is destructive self-love.

"My heart is broken over my daughter. My son is so good to me. He visits me every day and sees to it that I have plenty of groceries, and never misses calling me at night before he and his wife go to bed. But my daughter is just the opposite. Ever since my husband died, I have been so lonely, but do you think my daughter cares? Oh, she calls me two or three times a week, and drops in now and then. But I don't dare ask her to do me a favor. When I do, she grumbles and tells me it will do me good to get out and run the errand myself! I haven't wanted to go out at all since their father died. I'm much happier just to stay in the house. My son understands me, but my daughter doesn't."

I say the daughter does understand this woman and the son does not! No wonder she doesn't visit her mother more often (although, actually once or twice a week should be enough). After all, the daughter has a family of her own and a life of her own. This mother loves herself more than either child, and because she does, she puts her children in a strain over her. Mothers have to earn their children's love. Few seem to realize this, but it is true. And this is as it should be. After the child has left home, there can remain only *friendship*. This friendship can be the most beautiful of all, but a friendship must work two ways. When a woman just sits at home and waits for attention, those outside begin to dread her. It becomes a duty to "go by Mother's house." It should and can be a delight. I love my own mother more now than before my father died. She has left me free to love her! Our real friendship is one of my big joys.

This mother loves the way her children make her *feel*.

Real love has as its motivation genuine concern for the loved ones. The only difference between her son and her daughter is that she has the son cowed to submission. He is attentive to her to keep "peace."

We are to love and respect ourselves, but how can we respect the self that keeps other people in a strain? Real love *liberates*. This mother is not only binding her children, she is binding herself.

When Jesus raised Lazarus from the dead, He said: "Untie him, and give him a chance to move."

Self-love of the possessive, self-centered variety shackles the hearts and spirits and minds of those we "love." Are you tying someone in knots because you love yourself wrongly? If so, you are not only binding that person, you are binding yourself as well. And your *self* is meant to be free.

"If the Son shall make you free, you shall be free indeed."

Jesus meant this for everyone. This is why He longs for us to love ourselves enough and in the right way, so we will want to be free. This mother is bound heart and mind by the regularity or irregularity of the visits of her children.

Since my father has been gone, I have written at least a funny card to my mother almost every day. I don't do it because she expects it. I do it because I love her and think about her that often. If several days go by with no word from me, she does not feel neglected. She simply knows I'm busy and is glad. If anything were wrong, she would be notified. She knows I'm happiest when I'm busy, and because she loves *me* and wants the best for me, she doesn't sink into self-pity when I happen not to write to her for awhile. We are free to love each other *and* ourselves in our relationship. If I felt guilty and tied to this kind of regular correspondence, I would soon resent having to do it.

Real love *liberates*. And in the climate of liberty, love can grow.

A middle-aged couple had been going together for five years, with the idea of getting married. Then the gentleman involved began to back down. The woman almost lost her mind. "I love him, I love him!" she wailed. "He is my whole life. I want to take care of him and know that he is all right and after all this time of being so close, I don't see how he can suddenly grow cold toward me."

She had smothered him with possessive love and the wise gentleman acted in time to prevent a life-time of misery for them both. If she had been willing to see her wrongly directed love, perhaps they could have gone on with their marriage plans after awhile. She could not see, or she *would* not see that her "love" was entirely self-directed. She loved him because of the way *she felt* when she was with him. Her concern when he asked to postpone their marriage was not for him to find himself and be sure. It was for her *self*. *She* couldn't live without taking care of him. Three years have gone by and she is still trying to find someone to listen to her pathetic story.

I know of another similar case, only in this one the woman finally righted herself and began to pray for the man involved. Not that he would come back to her, but that his life without her would be good and fulfilling. They did not have the happy ending one would hope, but it is a creative ending, because both have grown enormously, and God is being allowed to heal the woman's broken heart.

She really loved this man. She really wanted the best for him. Perhaps she couldn't understand it all, but her God was big enough and real enough to attract her confidence. He knows all about handling and healing broken hearts.

Self-centered self love is rank *immaturity*. Children love themselves first of all. They love their parents according to how the parents make them *feel*. This is normal for them. The tragedy lies in the fact that this self-centered love which is normal for a child, shows up too often in adult men and women.

If you are *not*, first of all, concerned for the welfare and freedom of the person you think you love, then you are mistaken in your idea of real love. If you are constantly being hurt and slighted by someone, it is not because you love that person so much. It is because you love *you* in a self-protecting, egocentric way. You will suffer, if this is true, but perhaps not as much as those who really love you and hate the destructiveness of your misplaced self-love.

To love ourselves *rightly*, we must leave ourselves free to be whole persons in the midst of anything life can hand us. When we love and respect ourselves this way, we will have tapped the Source of love and will find ourselves able to give constructive, creative devotion to those whom God has given us to love.

To love ourselves *rightly*, we must love ourselves in God. We must respect ourselves as God's creation, and love ourselves as redeemed daughters of the King.

13: Understanding
Creative Love

13:

UNDERSTANDING CREATIVE LOVE

This can be the most important chapter in the entire book for you. The opening revelation of the need for every human being to *participate* in the very *creativity* of God is changing my own life daily. I find myself "entering in" as never before.

This kind of hourly participation in *creative love* is not easy. Participating with us in our sinful, earth-bound conduct is not easy for God. But God has never sought an easy way for Himself where we are concerned. He has simply gone on doing what had to be done for us, motivated only by His heart of love — never by our feeble progress toward His goals for us.

Participation in truly *creative love* is so difficult for us because it is so foreign to us. It was not foreign to our natures when God first created us. The first man and woman were "at home" in it, because they were *by nature*, at home with God Himself. The creature was comfortable with the Creator. In the sense that the creature was created in the Creator's own image, they were alike. They understood one another. They loved one another. They could communicate easily.

Then the creature jerked himself free from the Creator's care. By this act, the creature's very nature was changed. All that remained of the original alikeness was the haunting memory of the days when all was well in the Garden where God had placed His loved ones. The first man and woman were bereft! They missed Him painfully. All of life had become a brutal adjustment for them. Once they had laughed and danced among the beauties of their earthly paradise, as carefree as children and as interested in all the wonder about them. Now they dragged their newly wearied bodies through the days of hard work, their laughter turned hollow and their interest dulled to the mere acts of finding food and clothing.

In the beginning God had created for them a perfect environment, including all that was necessary for this man and woman to live fully through all the days of their intended eternal life on the beautiful planet where He placed them. The physical law of gravity, the right combination of hydrogen and oxygen molecules in the water they drank, the oxygen in the air they breathed, the miracle of the nitrogen cycle to keep the trees bearing and the grass green, the always returning sun at dawn and the night to make their rest deep — all this God created for man. And then He called it good. It was. All around him, God created the perfect environment for man to live to the ultimate of his capacity. A capacity so great no man has ever learned to enjoy it fully but God's Son, Jesus of Nazareth.

Without a doubt, the God who created the heavens and the earth and us, did His part to creative perfection. We are not concerned here with what man did to damage this creativity. (In the next chapter on "Understanding Redemptive Love" we will think on man's need for redemption.) For now, I wish to share with you what can truly change your entire approach to your own world in which you live.

First, you must recognize yourself as being (in one definite sense) the "creator" of the world around you. No matter what the disposition quirks and character failings of other people, you and I must face the fact that we do "create" an atmosphere around us. Only God is the lone Creator, but we are all little "creators" in that we create friction or peace, rest or strain, reality or "phoniness" in the area immediately surrounding us.

"I hate to see my husband come home at night," one woman said. "It's so peaceful all day long while he's at work. The children and I have a good time together, but the minute he puts his key in the front door the whole atmosphere of our home changes."

Now the big question. The one we must all face and answer, if we are to live through our problems to a place of real peace:

What kind of "world" are you creating around you?

Can you look at it and call it good? Or does this question make you shudder and want to hide? What kind of vibrations does your personality set up in your home? In the office where you work? In church? There is no possible chance of our being neutral here. We all "create" an atmosphere around us, and this atmosphere which we create is the "world" in which we expect our loved ones, our friends and associates, to live. How are the living conditions around you? Around me?

Are the people with whom we associate free to be their best selves? Are they free to be themselves at all, or are they always forced to consider us first?

"I have never been able to bring myself to share my apartment with anyone since the death of my dear friend who lived with me for so many years. She created such a good environment for me to 'grow in' that I find myself still growing because of it even after she's gone."

What a tribute to the memory of a woman! The atmosphere of her life was of such a caliber that its creative touch goes on after her death.

"She always left me free to think things out for myself, and I realize more each day without her that this is the way God loves us."

It is. God's love is all creative. God is the Creator. Everything about His personality promotes growth in us. He never stultifies or inhibits. Just as He moves within the tight little hard buds on a winter tree to interest them in spring, so He moves about and within the stunted human character to interest it in eternal life. And eternal life is not some future potential only, it is a quality of life available to everyone right now on this earth!

God created the conditions of life and growth when He created the altogether good environment for His loved ones, and then He committed Himself to nurturing their growth. Any human life can be a "watered garden." Watered by the very hand of the Creator Himself. Any human life can receive the warmth and energy from the One who called Himself the "light of the world."

God created the perfect environment "in the beginning" and He is still surrounding us with it in Jesus Christ. He can teach us how to create an environment which can be "called good" if we are willing.

What are some of the characteristics of the *creative love* of God?

One — it leaves us free to discover, to think, to decide, to act.

Two — it is sensitive to us, not pampering, but always letting us know we are *understood*.

Three — it encourages us, not only to bigger goals, but to complete honesty about our faults.

In all this, God's creative love gives us *room* always to move about!

"I am sure I have hurt my husband's Christian growth. He is a new Christian (two years) and in trying to help him, I have made it so uncomfortable for him in our home, he doesn't dare smoke or even read a magazine he thinks I might not approve of. I have always handled our money, and I am beginning to feel guilty about this too! Suddenly I can hear myself even trying to mold his thinking. If he doesn't like someone, I'm quick to correct him and remind him that we are supposed to love everyone if we are true followers of Jesus Christ. He is very good to me, but recently either seems to have no ideas of his own, or when he does, he shouts them at me. I think the thing that worries me most is this money business. He earns the living, and I'm afraid I've made him think he isn't capable of handling the money himself. Actually, he wasn't when we were mar-

ried, and this is one of the requirements I made when I said
'yes.' Now, I am wondering if I'm not being a bad influence
on him. It depresses me and makes me more anxious and I
don't know what to do."

I can only say "Hurrah!" This woman is going through
the first painful realization that her love is not only *uncre-
ative,* it is downright destructive to the moral fiber of this
man to whom she is married. But she is catching on! The
tragedy will end. Still, I see no other course of action for
her but to be utterly honest with her husband. She will
have to tell him what she told me, and rely on his mercy.
He is a Christian now and will have access to God's mercy.
If she has battered him so long, he can't forgive her immediately, she will just have to pray and wait.

God's environment (we could call it the "atmosphere
of heaven") always pushes back the barriers to growth and
development in us. God always gives us plenty of room.
Once more we go back to what Jesus said right after He
raised His friend Lazarus from the dead: "Untie him and
give him a chance to move."

A dear friend recently demonstrated this to me so
forcibly, I shall never be able to forget it. In a crisis time
in her life, she needed me to be strong and encouraging.
With all my heart I wanted to be, but the crisis seemed
sure to upset some work plans I had made. And try as I
surely did, I could do no more than barely control myself.
I gave her nothing and I knew it. She had every right to
be hurt with me, to suggest, at least, that I might try to give
her a little sympathy. She did none of this. Hours passed,
and I seemed to be withdrawing more and more into my
self-concerned shell. Finally, she put her arm around me
and said quietly, "I need you to be close to me now, but if
you can't be, I want you to know it's all right. Don't kick
yourself around."

My self-concerned shell splintered into fragments. In
a matter of a few minutes, I had "righted" myself, asked her
forgiveness and God's, and the friendship *gained* for eternity,
when it might have been permanently damaged.

What did she really do for me? She loved me *creatively*. I doubt that she stopped to analyze it that way, but Christ is her *life*, she is an authentic Christian. She *chose* at that moment, not to expound on her "rights." She had them, goodness knows, but He is a real presence to her, and she has seen the necessity for a mere human being *always* to choose to let Him lead in a tense situation like this. A woman does have this choice — men too, for that matter. My friend chose to love me with God's love. She gave me room to recover my perspective. She could have justifiably criticized me. Instead, she pushed back the walls of my struggle and reached toward me with *creative love*. She gave me both time and freedom to regain my balance. If she had criticized me, I would have defended myself and we would have been off on the "tangent" too familiar to us all.

If we are to understand creative love, we must understand that it draws on the very love of God in order to give the loved one freedom and room to *think through* the issues and return to reality. Creative love always preserves the *dignity* of the loved one. It never compromises or placates, but it always respects and reverences the other person's heart.

I was indulging myself in wrongly motivated self-love. My friend drew on the creative love of the God who cared desperately about us both at that moment. If she had chosen to demonstrate only self-love by accusing me, God would have lost the encounter. As it is, He won and we were both added to at the center of our beings. You may not be as fortunate as I was to have someone else who will try *creative love* with you the next time there is a disturbance. But *you* can try it with someone. I promise it will be an experience you will both never be able to forget.

Theories are stimulating, but the actual experience of participating in creative love makes it uniquely *ours*. And once we are in possession of it by way of our understanding, we find the opening revelation going on. We become the owners of new patience. We find being kindled within ourselves new interest in the feelings and reactions of those around us. We move gradually, but surely from limiting subjectivity toward the open objectivity of God. We now and then seem in reality to be seeing things from His viewpoint. Old prejudices are suddenly nowhere to be found.

An "entered into" experience of creative love is in a sense another conversion. We gasp in surprise at how narrow we were, how immune to large human sympathies. We want to weep bitterly over our once calloused hearts. Instead, we laugh with the joy of feeling our hearts growing tender with new understanding, new respect and new reasonableness.

One of the strong characteristics of the human life turned creative, by having entered into the actual practice of creative love, is new *reasonableness*. Not only do we find ourselves being more reasonable, we find ourselves more willing to try to reason with other people. Once more we want to weep over our old stubbornness. Instead, we sigh with relief that we discover ourselves able to weigh matters realistically and discriminate between real and imagined slights and wrongs.

We discover more of the nature of God when we enter actively into the practice of creative love. We plumb some of the depths of His words: "Come now . . . and let us reason together."

If God invites His creatures with "sins like scarlet" to *reason* with Him, how can we dare to remain haughty and unreasonable?

When we dare to practice creative love, we find an unsuspected store of humility within ourselves. "I am meek and lowly in heart," Jesus said of Himself. We now find no more use for the old false "humility." We have found more of Him, and we have found His humility within ourselves, where He has been waiting for our willingness to discover it.

He is there, living within you now. He has been there ever since you received Him as your Saviour. He is the Creator God as well as the Saviour God, and the experience of participating in His creative love toward someone is yours any time you decide to "enter in."

The experience of "entering in" may be waiting for you soon. Crisis times come to us all. If the Holy Spirit has whetted your desire for an experience of creative love, you can now anticipate the next crisis, instead of dreading it. But remember, you must watch your *timing*. Creative love is never experienced from sudden impulsive actions. God "took His time" when He created the heavens and the earth. If a family row looms, don't jump in without thinking. And please do your thinking conscious that you are in *His presence*. The time to think may be only a few seconds, if the words have already begun to fly. But our God is not limited by the second hands on our watches and clocks. It is always *now* with Him. He can give you His attitude in an instant, if you have come to feel at home with Him. You will recognize His voice, if you have made it a habit to listen.

This is no technique I advocate. It is an attitude of receptivity toward the Creator God, and this is usually not cultivated in a day. The only time limit is set by us, however. Our willingness is the tempo-maker. You and I can long for an experience of creative love, but block it with a hasty word spoken from an unwilling heart.

I hope your heart is willing.

I hope also that you see now, why the chapter on "Understanding Self-love" had to precede this one. Until we can distinguish between right and wrong self-love, we cannot possibly get at the redemptive heart of *creative love*. In the next chapter, we will be exposing ourselves to some possible new understanding of *redemptive love*.

For now, may I urge you to re-read the Creation story in the book of Genesis in your Bible? Read it this time asking the Holy Spirit of the same God who created, to show you *in your own circumstances*, the real nature of creative love. Ask Him to teach you how to apply it with your family, your friends or the people with whom you work.

Surely, it is not enough that we merely believe that "In the beginning God created the heavens and the earth." We must go much farther than that. We must allow Him to stir us up to an active interest in learning how to make use of creative love hour by hour during our stay on the earth He created for us. During this earth-life, we may never learn how to make perfect use of His love, but we can learn to feel at home with it. And when you and I feel at home with the love of God, other people will begin to be at home with us.

We are certainly responsible to God for the kind of "world" we create for those loved ones of His whom He has given us. God needs us to "give His love" to everyone!

14: Understanding
Redemptive Love

14:

UNDERSTANDING REDEMPTIVE LOVE

If there had been a way to make Chapter 13 and Chapter 14 one, I would have done it. We must have it clear in our minds that *redemptive* love is not a different or separate thing from *creative* love. One is merely a continuation of the other.

They spring together from the same Heart.

Both are characteristic of God Himself. They are the two sides of the same love. He is forever involved with both. This cannot change, because God cannot change.

"Thou art the same; thy years shall never end."

With all His heart God wanted His creatures once again to be able to enjoy the *creative love* experienced by the first man and woman before their disobedient act against His love. He wanted this so much, He set His *redemptive* love in operation even before they fled the Garden! As the two newly sinful creatures stood, still shuddering in the fresh shame of their nakedness, God shouted to their tempter: "I will put enmity between you and the woman; also between your offspring and her offspring: He will crush your head and you will crush His heel!"

This first mention by the Lord God of the coming Someone who would crush the head of the enemy of His beloved creatures, came — not before, not after — but exactly when it was needed. A tiny seed of hope must have sprung

157

to life in the darkened, frightened, shame-filled hearts of Adam and Eve. They couldn't have understood it, but God had spoken, and so they must have hoped at least.

Someone would come. He would come from God Himself, and He would be the bearer of God's *redemptive* love. He would take this horrible thing that happened in paradise, and somehow, in some way (known only in the counsels of the high God), would *redeem* — not only the dreadful act of mankind, but mankind himself.

We know this in retrospect now, because He *has come*.

His name was Jesus of Nazareth, the Son of God. He was the "offspring of a woman" — Mary, the simple, clear-hearted Hebrew girl. He was born to Mary in the normal way, but He was conceived by the Holy Spirit of God Himself.

"He came from God . . ." He was one with the Father.

Isaiah, his heart tuned surely to the heart of God, gave the good news of His coming to the depressed Israelites, as though He had already arrived: "For to us a Child is born, to us a Son is given: the government shall be upon His shoulder; and His name shall be called Wonderful, Counselor, the Mighty God, Everlasting Father, the Prince of Peace."

He came, just as Isaiah had said He would. Just as God Himself had promised in the Garden that dark, tragic day when His creatures first disobeyed His loving command. When He came, even the simple shepherds watching their sheep on the hillside outside the little city of Bethlehem heard the angels themselves singing out the good news: "Glory to God in the highest, and on earth *peace* among men of His favor!"

Beside a straw-filled manger, down in the town of Bethlehem, Mary, the young wife of faithful Joseph, was at that moment wrapping her Baby in swaddling clothes, her heart filled with a wonder she dared not try to express in words.

He came, just as God said He would. This Redeemer, who would "save His people from their sins." This Jesus

Christ, the *only* begotten Son of God. He came, and He grew to manhood in the hill-town of Nazareth, and then He left His mother's home and began to live out in every word and every action, the *redemptive love* of God. The compassion in His heart toward every human affliction would have shattered the mental and physical health of an ordinary man. This was no ordinary man. This was the God-Man, sent from the Father.

"I and the Father are one," He said. "If you have seen Me, you have seen the Father."

Shocking words. A shocking life. He stunned the men dulled by earthly power, with the claims He made about Himself. They honestly believed Him to be blaspheming against the Lord God. His poise shocked them. His strength angered them. His gentleness mocked them. His love condemned them. He did not condemn them, but the purity and intensity and constancy of His love caused men to do one of two things: Either they turned their hearts to follow Him, or they began to plot ways to do away with Him! The very light of God pierced deep into their hearts when they stood in His presence. Men lost control of themselves. They either surrendered this control into His loving hands, or they tore their garments in their frantic efforts to get rid of Him once and for all.

For three days they thought they had made it. His quiet, unbroken strength (almighty meekness) fanned their fury as they stood watching the heavy nails pierce His hands and feet, when the Roman soldiers secured Him to His cross. He was taking into His heart the very sin that motivated His persecutors, as He hung there, but they could not know this. Their hearts and minds were blinded by that sin. The same dark, inner drive which prodded the first man and woman toward the forbidden tree to satisfy their desire to know as much as God knew. In the heart of each man who plotted His death, there twisted the tormentor whom God hated. He did not hate these murderers, He hated the disease that had made them murderers. As the God-Man hung above them, praying for them, He loved them with the *kind* of love that could have healed them on the spot!

"Father, forgive them, because they know not what they are doing."

Down from His cross poured *redemptive love* in quantity enough for the whole human race. Enough for you. Enough for me. Far from decreasing because of our behavior against Him, it seemed rather to increase. The same situation still exists today and will exist as long as the earth stands.

The outstanding characteristic of redemptive love is *perseverance*. God never gives up. The more sin He sees in us, the more He bathes us in His redemptive love. Why? Because He knows nothing else will heal us!

Redemptive love never protects itself, as Jesus did not protect Himself from the cross. In all ways, under all circumstances, it reaches, reaches toward the loved ones, to heal — to redeem. No one is out of its reach. The Bible tells us that "the Lamb was slain before the foundation of the world." To me, this means that God did not suddenly become a redemptive God as Jesus hung on His cross, pouring out His very life blood for everyone. It means that God's love has always been *redemptive* as well as *creative*. It means that before He "created the heavens and the earth," before He created man, God *knew* what we would do. What we would force Him to do. And knowing, He still went right on creating. As Adam and Eve enjoyed their perfect life during those first days in the Garden, God did not enjoy it with them any less because He knew what they were going to force Him to do — but He did know.

If you are in close communion and at peace with Him today, He knows what you may do next week; but this does not decrease His joy in you now. "He will joy over you with singing" — still knowing you as you are because He knows the power and sees the end results of *redemptive love*.

This is *something* of the nature of God's redemptive love toward us. Knowing as He does, "what is in man," He continues in His own love toward us. He did not "try" *creative love* first, and seeing that it failed, suddenly switch to *redemptive love.* "The Lamb *was* slain before the foundation of the world." God knew all along.

Quite recently a minister said to me: "I know this is true, and I'm sure you've heard it said a hundred times that God does not hate the sinner, only his sin. But this is a very hard concept for me to understand."

Of course it is. And it is not understandable at all unless we come to see that *creative love* and *redemptive love* are in reality two sides of the same God-heart.

Our human love, at its highest and most *creative,* cannot always love the person whose personality has been twisted by sin. Especially, if that "twist" is directed toward us! But human love can be invaded by the *redemptive* love of the God of the cross, and can function redemptively under the most difficult circumstances.

I once read of a family of four people, who have sufficiently experienced the redemptive love of God in their lives, so that they are living it out daily under circumstances that would make the average (merely "saved") Christian wince. In this family is the mother, the father and the sister of a boy who was shot *after capture* by a Japanese soldier. The young Japanese boy was simply twisted at the center of his being by the fury of war. He did not need to shoot the American boy. His prisoner was unarmed and marching with a dozen others toward a prison camp. Somehow the details of the killing reached the dead boy's parents. It took three years following the war to work out the arrangement, but the fourth *member* of that family now, is the Japanese boy who pulled the trigger of the rifle that killed their son! This family recognized the Japanese boy, not as an enemy, but as a disturbed, frenzied victim of the chaotic world their generation had handed him. They took him in as their own son. It happened that his parents were killed at Hiroshima, and this thoroughly Christian family saw the glorious opportunity to "fill in behind the sufferings of Christ." The glorious opportunity to demonstrate true *redemptive love.*

I maintain that they could not have done this under the power of mere human love, even at its best. They were

Christian believers, who believed themselves to have been in the same sin-distorted condition as the boy who killed their son — until they met the Saviour. In reality, no one can see or practice redemptive love, until he sees himself as just another person equally in need of a Saviour.

Several years ago, when I was still writing the radio program, "Unshackled," we dramatized the tremendously redemptive story of the conversion of a derelict woman of the streets named Mattie Rice. Mattie lived back in the days following the turn of our century, when Chicago's downtown streets still had wooden side-walks. She drank so heavily, and was so destitute, that she often slept, clutching her bottle, under the wooden sidewalks of the Skid Row area.

For months, the staff of the Pacific Garden Mission, then under the supervision of Colonel and Mrs. Clark, its founders, had prayed for poor Mattie. At last, one night she half fell through the doors of the Mission chapel, still clutching her bottle. Her hair hung in her eyes, her skin was coated with filth, she had lost most of her teeth, and her hands were so swollen she could scarcely hold the big quart bottle. Mattie stood there swaying unsteadily, looking around the warm, gas-lit chapel. At the door, greeting everyone who came in, stood dainty, ex-socialite Mrs. Clark. The two women looked at each other for a long moment. Mattie could stand the silence no longer and shouted: "Well, whata' ya' gonna' do with me?"

Mrs. Clark moved quickly toward the hideous woman. "I'm going to kiss you, Mattie. I'm so glad to see you!"

The redemptive love of Christ poured through Mrs. Clark to Mattie. The remaining years of her life were spent working in a mission station with children in the hills of Kentucky.

Mrs. Clark knew the "plan of salvation" and could have pointed out all the "right" Scriptures. This would not have been enough for Mattie Rice that night. The *redemptive love* of the Saviour she so desperately needed had to be demonstrated.

Man had all the Scriptures of the Old Testament, before Jesus came. But God knew the *redemptive love* of His own heart had to be demonstrated. And so He came Himself, in the person of Jesus Christ, to show us once and for all His great, eternal consuming desire to bring us back into a peaceful relationship with Himself.

I believe we can say that while both creative and redemptive love are equally characteristic of the nature of His heart, God knew that He had to demonstrate His *redemptive love*, before we would even catch on how to participate in His *creative love*. God is the Creator God, but as long as we are cut off from Him by our very natures, we cannot "enter in" creatively with Him. There is only one way to be reunited with Him, because there is only one way to discover one's need to be — and that is to examine the whole human dilemma in the light of the *identity* of the One who hung on the cross of Calvary.

What kind of environment are you creating around you?

Are you able to show creative love? Are you able to push back the obstacles to honesty *for* other members of your family? For your friends? Are you able to sit quietly (without fighting) in touch with God, *participating* in His understanding of the real causes of the trouble surrounding that person? Are you able to let self-defense go in *reverence* for the need of the other person involved in the difficulty? Can you *identify* with him or with her?

If not, then perhaps you need to be quiet before the Saviour who redeemed you, in order to give His Spirit a chance to show you once and for all *why* you, too, needed to be redeemed! No member of the human race needs redemption any more than another. Without a doubt, we are all "beggars" before God. But His redemptive love *preserves our human dignity*, even at the moment of darkest shame.

Redemptive love was operative at that dark moment in the Garden, too. God was preserving the human dignity of His sinful children. They were ashamed of their disobedience, and the shame manifested itself in self-consciousness over their nakedness. But "The Lord God made robes of skins for Adam and for his wife and clothed them."

Even there, the great Heart of love reached *toward* them.

Mere skins to cover their nakedness would not be enough, though. God knew this. These people needed a Redeemer. God knew also that even the Redeemer would not be able to touch their darkened hearts unless He came in a way which anyone could understand. No remote, exalted, powerful monarch can find entrance into a fear-ridden, darkened human heart.

Mattie Rice did not need a Bible expositor standing above her in a polished pulpit the night she staggered into the Skid Row Mission. She needed another human being to *identify* with her! For a moment, at least, Mrs. Clark *experienced* something of the agony that was Mattie Rice. She bothered to let Mattie know it. The gentle, refined lady "got into" the trouble with Mattie.

God bothered to do the same thing with us, when He came to this earth *as one of us*. He "got into" the trouble with us.

Redemptive love receives us as we are, and then begins to heal us. Healing comes, I imagine, both from redemptive and creative love, because healing comes from the total heart of God. He doesn't reserve any grudging areas for Himself.

We, however, as far as I can see, cannot show true, consistently creative love until we have learned more of the nature of the redemptive love of God toward us as individual women.

"All of his life, I tried to run my son's affairs for him," one lady wrote. "God showed me my terrible sin! And He showed me so clearly, that I now am able to *be patient* with my son while he gradually recovers from his resentment toward me for being the way I was for so many years."

This woman saw that for her to change in her domineering attitude toward her son was *not enough*. God had shown His patient, redemptive love toward her so clearly, that she was then *able* to show patience toward her son while he was ridding himself of his resentment toward her.

The experience and increased knowledge of the nature of God's *redemptive love* enabled her to show *creative love* to her son. She was able to create an atmosphere around him in which he could recover from his resentment in his own way, according to his personality. We don't all snap back at the same speed. Some of us just move more slowly than others. Truly creative love always pushes back the barriers to give the other person room to recover.

The doctrine of redemption is a dead thing unless we allow it to become a part of us. Anyone can receive the redemptive love of God. But we all need to *understand* it more practically. And there is no way to make a discovery yours more certainly than to try it out in your daily living.

Our God says, "Be not afraid, for I have redeemed you; I have called you by your name; you are Mine."

This is true. He has redeemed us, if we have linked our lives with His, but He now has a right to expect us to remember that He does know our names, where we live, and how we act with those we know. He has a right to expect us to remember what our redemption cost Him. And the best way to let Him know that we remember is to be willing to give both His creative and redemptive love to those around us under all circumstances. We can't give creative love one day and redemptive love the next. They *cannot* be separated. But just suppose God could and would do this with us! Suppose one day, He just sat back and said, "Now, go it on your own today. After all, did I not create you and give you all your blessings? Today, just obey Me and worship Me as your Creator God alone. Today, I am withholding My redemptive love."

Where would we be if He did this? Only He knows. But He also knows that we cannot make it successfully and creatively *without* redemptive love. He knows we need a fresh supply every day, too. He has the supply. He cannot turn off either His creative love or His redemptive love because He cannot extinguish Himself. Where God is — love is. Because God is love.

15: Growing Up to Peace

15:

GROWING UP TO PEACE

Jesus told us we were to become like little children. But He did not say we were to be *childish*. The dictionary will tell you that *childlike* is a different thing from *childish*. Childlike implies "childlike obedience, submissiveness." To be childish denotes a state of mind "pertaining to childhood, immature, silly; not fit for an adult."

There is a whole world of difference between the two words when applied to an adult. A childlike adult is obedient, meek, trusting. This is what Jesus meant. He did not say child*ish*, He said "except you become *like* a little child." And He was speaking of trusting God.

We have shared together now, through fourteen chapters of stating problems and consequences; of discussing God's ultimate solution to those problems. We have attempted to show that God does know about and have a definite way for us to *live through our problems from confusion to peace*. I have tried to let you know that I, too, share some of the same basic problems with you. I have also tried to communicate to you some of my insights into His willingness to see us through these problems. In fact, I thought of ending the book with the chapter you have just read on His *redemptive love*.

The answer lies there, beyond the shadow of a doubt.

Still, I feel we need to be more specific — more practical. St. Paul, of course, was a great believer in getting down to real causes. He was an intensely brilliant but also an

169

intensely practical man. He had been given the difficult assignment by God, not only to reach the pagan world for Jesus Christ, but to teach them how to *grow up* in their new lives. This was no harder then than it is now. It is also no harder now than it was then.

First of all, let's face the fact that all eight of the basic problems with which we dealt at length (a chapter for each) *are* directly the problems of *immaturity*. The problems of *doubt, ingratitude, ignorance, darkness, extremism, conditioning, busyness and competition* — all spring from a basic immaturity within us.

The problems found in children are normal — to children. The same problems found in adults are abnormal. It is normal for a child to doubt and be afraid and to lean on his parents. Children seldom remember to be grateful, to say "thank you" unless an adult reminds them. Gratitude is not natural with children. They are *normally* still in the stage where they have a right to expect to get things. Children are ignorant and in darkness simply because they have not been around long enough to have had a chance to learn. It is normal for children to be extremists. If a child likes candy, he is simply being a normal child when he tries to get hold of the whole box! Children are quite naturally motivated by their conditioning. If a certain thing is done or said at home, it is perfectly natural for the child to do or say this thing away from home. Children are always busy. "My goodness, Mary, can't you sit still for five minutes?" Of course this sounds familiar. They do not know how to budget their time. They're not supposed to know. They're still children. Competition is sometimes quite violent among even very small children and normally so. Anyone or anything that threatens the child's security automatically becomes the child's rival.

Every problem we stated is *normally* a problem of childhood. The parent and teacher face the task of teaching the child how to learn to control himself in these problem areas. This is simply "training the child in the way that he should go." But having these problem areas is not a bad thing in a child. It is natural because of the child's age.

Now pay attention to St. Paul, who has some perceptive and definite things to say when these same problems of childhood disturb grown-up people!

"When I was a child I talked as a child: I entertained child interests; I reasoned like a child; but on becoming a man I was through with childish ways."

This potent bit of advice Paul wrote to the new church at Corinth. Apparently they had as many adults in the church nursery as we still have today. To the church at Ephesus, he also wrote, "We should no longer be babes, swung back and forth and carried around with every changing whiff of teaching that springs from human cunning and ingenuity for devising error; but, lovingly attached to truth, we should *grow up* in every way toward Him who is the Head — Christ. . . ."

Since this book concerns us as women and *our choice* in the matter of whether we are to be willing to take God's way out of our problems from confusion to peace, it might be well to paraphrase the first statement we quoted from Paul to the church at Corinth. (It takes very little paraphrasing too!) Read it aloud:

"When I was a little girl, I talked as a little girl; I entertained little girl interests; I reasoned like a little girl; but on becoming a woman, I was through with little girl ways."

Well? How did it sound to you when you heard your own voice reading these often glossed-over lines from the end of the familiar Corinthian love chapter?

Do you still talk like a little girl? That is, do you speak before you think? Do you know what you're talking about before you say the words, or do you just chatter thoughtlessly and aimlessly the way a little girl does?

Do you speak from knowledge or from ignorance? Do you speak from God-given insight about both divine and human nature? Or do you prattle without waiting quietly before God for His sure word concerning the situation, the scripture or the person involved? Do you speak from inner fear and doubt as a little girl has a right to do? Or do you speak from inner confidence, built into your heart as a result of time spent with the God who has promised to care

for you? Do you speak caustically or carelessly — the words
springing haphazardly from the extremist side of your
nature? Are you rigid and unyielding because like a little
girl, you have just taken someone else's word for a matter
and haven't bothered to think it through yourself? Are you
thoughtless, even cruel, because you have been so busy with
your own little doings you have forgotten how to think
before you speak? Are you quick to cut someone down to
size because that person somehow seems to have bested you
in a real or imagined competition?

Little girls do all these things and it is normal for them
to do them.

You and I are women. We are no longer little girls —
in years, at least. It is not only immature and un-Christian,
it is downright ridiculous for harsh, thoughtless, cutting
words to come from the mouth of a woman on whose face
are the marks of her years! Years that should have proven
to her (if her mirror hasn't) that it is time to *grow up.*

How do you talk? Like a little girl? Or like the woman
you are now?

"When I was a little girl . . . I *entertained* child
interests."

What does this mean? Little girls are always, first and
last, interested in themselves. Once more, for them, it is
normal. What about us at 25, 35, 50, 60, 70 and more? What
kind of interests are we to entertain?

Are we to entertain our doubts? Are we to entertain
our feelings of ingratitude by continuing to tell ourselves
we are too precious for life to treat us this way? Are we to
entertain our ignorance and our spiritual darkness by refusing to use the minds God gave us to read and study? Are
we to entertain the imbalance of our natures by coddling
our extremes? By insisting upon perfection either in ourselves or in someone else? By over-eating or over-talking
or pressing home our opinions as children almost always do
unless someone silences them? Are we to go on entertaining
our rigidly conditioned minds by flying in the face of every
new idea because it isn't what mother (or the pastor) said it
should be? Are we to go on feeling martyrs while adding to

our already crowded schedules with no more balance or
perceptivity than little Mary when she is playing house one
minute and making mud pies the next? Are we going to
entertain the competitive spirit within ourselves by self-
defense and constant self-reference?

How about it, dear sisters? Where do you and I stand
here? Have we put away little girl entertainments? Or are
we brazenly disobeying God's Word to "grow up in *every
way* toward Him?"

"When I was a little girl, I *reasoned* like a little girl."

I doubt if we need to go through the list of eight problems again here. What about your reasoning? Is it always
toward you or in your behalf? If so, then you are a "little
girl" emotionally, at *your* age. If everything we approach is
approached in respect or in deference to our viewpoint, or
from the viewpoint of what it will do to make us look better
or seem more spiritual or bring us the biggest return in
money, praise or downright flattery or convenience, then —
we are little girls in our reasoning.

The widowed mother mentioned in an earlier chapter,
who was making life a chaos for her daughter, was showing
a most glaring kind of immaturity. She was saying in effect,
"Here I am, lonely and widowed and now what are you
going to do about me?"

The little girl runs to her mother crying, "I fell down
and broke my doll and now I don't have a doll to play with,
do something about me!"

Please do not think (if your heart has been recently
broken by the loss of your loved one) that I am being cal-
lous about widowhood. I have experienced the agonizing
adjustment as closely as I can experience it, with my own
mother. But the fact remains that life does knock us all
down, and if we are mature Christians, we do not run crying
to the nearest relative or friend demanding that she or he
do something about us!

God's creative love is in full operation *toward* you, if
you are a widow, or lonely for any reason. His love is not
only in motion toward you, it is trying with all the great
energy of the heart of God Himself, to *invade* your heart.

God is calling to you right now, "I need you. I need you to begin to *participate* with Me in this creative love of Mine." Creativity is uniquely natural with women. The widowed woman, or the woman left alone for any reason, has a glorious opportunity to "enter in" with God in creating a new life. Not only for herself. This will soon begin to seem almost incidental. But she has free time, with plenty of energy to participate with Him in bringing to other people some of this creative love He longs to give.

When we are suddenly alone and frightened and grief-stricken, the temptation to return to our "little girl ways" is enormous. God knows about the pain and the loneliness and the grief, but He also knows you will become only a *problem creator* unless you are willing by His grace to "grow up" in this, too.

My mother has not only (in full cooperation with God) created a new life for herself and those around her in the city where she lives, she has (more than she realizes) created a new, carefree life for me, too.

If these lines seem hard to take, be sure the *creative* and the *redemptive* love of God surrounds you in them.

"When I was a little girl, I *reasoned* like a little girl."

A woman with whom I recently spoke, was doing just that. "My husband just decided after we had been married fifteen years that he would up and leave me! I used to be an outgoing person — I worked in the church, I visited the sick, I kept a neat house. Now that he's gone, I can't bring myself to do anything. I can't even leave the house."

No one doubts the special, unique agony of a woman in circumstances like these. But this woman has used her tragedy as an excuse to begin reasoning once more like a little girl. Her reason has fallen to pieces, in fact. Either this, or she is on the brink of a glorious discovery: Could it have been that she was an outgoing person, who worked in the church, visited the sick, and kept a nice house because she was in fortunate circumstances with a husband to care for her? Didn't Jesus Christ enter into her busy picture anywhere? Children never stop to examine their motives.

We must. Realistically examining our true motive is the basis for adult reasoning.

The same basis for adult reasoning (growing up) applies as well to those of us who are single and earn our own living. Our problems differ somewhat outwardly, but basically I believe the ultimate answers are the same. We, too, need to be realistic not only in our motives but in the way we accept our lives.

"You don't seem to mind being single at all," one embittered woman in her forties wrote. "But I hate it, and although I am a good secretary, I am unfulfilled. Every day the same old grind, the same old chores every night and everything is up to me!"

She sounds as resentful as the woman who kicked at the walls of her "prison" of motherhood and domesticity, doesn't she?

"You may be happy," she continued, "but if you really are, it must be because you are a writer and have a little creative activity."

I have long believed that the single woman who works is so often restless and rebellious mainly because she is unfulfilled creatively. What wonders might take place in how many offices and stores and schools across the world if only the *Christian* career women began to participate in the creative love of God?

Just before I began the writing of this chapter, a stimulating full page report of a conclave conducted by the *Chicago Tribune* writer, Mary Maryfield, supported this thinking. Miss Maryfield interviewed members of the Chicago Business and Professional Women's Clubs on tape, and here are some of their viewpoints:

"I believe a single woman with a good job should be the world's happiest woman — if she'd just give up looking for something that isn't there."

"We keep dreaming of some kind of creative work because of frustrated self-realization. Maybe that's why the majority of us here said our *secret dream was to write!*"

This makes sense, doesn't it? Not that all working women should suddenly attempt to become writers, but the reasoning is adult and sound. Women, in particular, were intended to *participate* in *creativity*. When a woman spends her life working for a man who is not her own, often with insufficient appreciation shown for her efforts, she naturally feels frustrated and unfulfilled. Could it be that she is using her job as a substitute and then complaining because it can never *be* an adequate substitute?

"What good does it do to gripe about our jobs *or* our bosses?" This from a Christian professional woman I know who has the picture straight in its frame of mature thinking. "We complain about missing the joys of motherhood and a husband, but what good does it do? I don't have a husband and I don't have children, so why increase the tension around me by boring other people with it? I just go along enjoying the outside activities I find time for, believing that the God I follow knows all about my situation. He does, too! And as long as I cooperate with Him, I don't find my life empty or unfulfilled. It might not be filled with the things I'd have chosen for myself, but it's still a good life and He keeps me as busy and interested as any married woman I know. This is where I am, and I intend to make the most of it!"

This woman has *grown up* emotionally. She is accepting her life with joy and she is loved and needed. Most of the circumstances of a woman's life — career woman or housewife — cannot be changed outwardly. But we can be changed within those circumstances when we are at last willing to grow up to the viewpoint of God.

Our God is a Creator-God and He has as many ways for allowing us to participate with Him in creative living as there are women in the world who need to participate.

If we have truly put away childish things, if we are really through with them, we face facts as they are. Children face facts as they wish they were, not as they are. This kind of mature viewpoint will increase the capacity for peace in any woman — young or old, professional woman or housewife. It will move us steadily and creatively through the routine days and through the crisis times. *We discover how to lay hold of peace as we discover the freedom of maturity.*

I have come to know and love a young lady in her early twenties, as I have watched her "grow up in every way toward Christ" during the tremendously difficult and humiliating two years just past. She needed someone to see the great potential in her. Other Christians had been shaming her for what she had done; alternately forcing her to "still more" repentance and then "casting out the devil" they decided was in her. My heart ached for her, but I saw the glorious opportunity for *creative love*. My own sense of His *redemptive love* in my life made it all joy to show His creative love to this intelligent, deeply troubled girl.

She had done a shocking thing (particularly shocking to the kind of Christian who has never known the freedom which can come from having shocked oneself!). She *was* in trouble. I saw her here in Chicago just a few days before the legal hearing, which could easily implicate her in a further difficulty of which she was innocent. The girl was honest before God, but frightened half to death. To give her something constructive to do during the waiting time, I asked her to write down every day (for use in this book) whatever came to her to write. It is not intended to be great writing and it holds no "spiritual phoniness." Some of the days are black only. Here is her journal as she sent it to me later:

June 4. My problem today is loneliness in my trouble. I went for a long walk. Three hours. Bought magazines and a newspaper. Read a lot. Afraid to think ahead. Trying to live just today.

June 5. Reading Anna Mow's book, *Say Yes to Life!* Thought this would help more than magazines. It saved the day. This day. This living for just today — just for the moment — is actually the simplest sounding but hardest thing to do. Yet, Jesus said to do it. I try so hard to obey this. But I can't.

June 6. Rough day. Didn't read Anna Mow's book today. Watched TV. It's hard to do anything but think of my own situation. I *force* myself to keep busy at something. And I mean *force*. There must be something I'm doing wrong. I keep feeling like I'm running from something. I'm innocent of the charges coming up at the hearing and I've cleared my own "mistakes." Yet I want to run, run, run, run. Don't think. Don't think. Run. Am I running from myself? From my *immature* childish self?

June 7. Started this day right — with the Lord! If I'm still a baby, only He can "grow me up." Why don't I consciously spend more time with Him? It seems the only thing that keeps me from going to pieces. Sometimes I've been very conscious of His Presence with me. I mustn't be *childish* and expect to *feel* Him here all the time. He said He would be. A week to wait yet for the hated hearing. I'm scared sometimes. Really.

June 8. When I'm at work I feel pretty good. There I go with that infantile stuff again about how I feel. But my feelings show more than my faith! What's happening to me? I'm innocent — I can prove it. He was my boy-friend, but not when he did what he did. I had broken it off with him and I can prove that. I feel all stirred up down inside — sometimes like I really *want* to be thinking about the danger at the hearing! How can I be so goofy? I actually seem as though I want to think about the things that depress me. I love horseback riding, so that occupied my evening hours.

June 9. Didn't do much to help myself today. Television. More television. I feel numb.

June 10. Today I am forcing myself to replace every worried thought with a *thank you* to Jesus. I am much quieter inside. But still numb. So much of what I'm doing seems self-effort. How could this ever help anyone in your book, Genie? I must be doing something wrong during this waiting period. There seems to be an *upward pull* — but how do I take hold? I know He is with me.

June 11. Today I've approached this situation in a new way. This morning first thing, I said, "Lord — here, it's Your problem today. I give it to You as a gift. Now *You* keep it all day, so I can rest from it." And you know something? I was much better all day.

June 12. Maybe I'm growing up a tiny bit anyway! I decided one thing today. Not that I think TV is sinful, but for me now, during this trying period of waiting for the hearing, it's out! Only an idiot would keep on filling her mind with all those crime stories when she's trying to keep her mind off a hearing of her own. I have to begin to use the *reason* and sense God gave me! The side of my nature that got me into trouble frightens me. Why cultivate it? "Let this mind be in you that was in Jesus Christ." Oh, if I only knew how to do that. I just keep giving this whole mess to Jesus, asking Him to redeem it! Is this the right thing to do?

June 13. The day draws nearer. So near it is — tomorrow! I notice I don't seem to feel much of anything today. Almost no feeling or emotion. Not that I don't care if I get cleared. I do. But I don't feel much of anything, even God. Maybe He is numbing me so I can hold together. Anyway, I am going to be grown up about this and trust Him! I'm not going to panic!

June 14. The hearing is over. I did not panic. I just went through it telling the truth and still feeling numb. I don't even feel much relief. Somehow I feel more interested in what God will do with me *now*.

June 15. I know I was to write this only up to the hearing. But it suddenly seems almost incidental to
what is happening inside me. I am confused at
the part of me that made me do what I did —
shocked and hurt by it. Grateful to be free and
declared innocent of the last trouble, but *most
interested* in some new stirring inside me for
tomorrow now that Jesus is growing real to
me and not just the executor of the plan of
salvation! He and I can live together every day,
can't we? I don't need to be in trouble to know
He's with me! I finished reading Anna Mow's
book — it has surely been a life-saver! I am learning that my *peace* is not where I am living or
where I am working or whether or not I get out
of trouble. Could it be true that Jesus Christ
really *is* our peace, the way Paul said? Yes, it
is true! I am not going to be a baby and with-
draw to myself, for fear of more condemnation.
I am going out with my head up and learn to
laugh again with people. I must learn to control my thoughts. One negative thought *entertained* and I'm sunk. I am refusing myself
absolutely the luxury of self-pity or panic! Hey,
could I be really *growing up* at last?

Yes, she is growing up like a bright, strong shoot right
out of the heart of God Himself! This girl is one of my big
joys.

I try sometimes to imagine how she must fill the heart
of God with a joy only He can bear. None of her growing
up process has been easy. You can read pain and fear for
yourself, and as she told me, she only wrote briefly every
day. She has "entered in" by way of the cross of her Lord
Jesus and is now *participating creatively* in the freedom
to be found only when we allow our lives to grow up and
out from the heart of God — as my friend is doing.

Did you notice that her little journal ended on the
note that "He is our *peace*"? Did you notice her references
to the fact that she was "growing up"? These two facts are

so inter-twined, they cannot be separated. In my book, *Early Will I Seek Thee* (Fleming H. Revell Co.), I said peace does not come in a package from God. Peace is God Himself. "He (Jesus Christ) *is* our peace."

We have no choice but to *grow up to peace*. This is exactly what Paul meant when he wrote, ". . . we should grow in every way toward Him. . ."

You and I have faced at least eight of the basic *immaturity* areas shared by all of us. Basic problems which block us from the joy of living for which Christ gave His life. Remember, He did not mean only some distant state of bliss, when He gave Himself on His cross for our eternal life. Eternal life does begin *now*. You and I can live through our problems from the confusion of our battered emotions and misplaced sympathies, to peace.

We can learn to understand the real issues involved in our problems and we can learn to understand ourselves in them. We can, by grace, extend this understanding to the people whose "world" we create.

We must be willing to think maturely. Paul said this to the Corinthians, too: ". . .you must not be children in your thinking. . . you should think maturely!"

Only the unrealistic woman will fancy that the way provided by God for her to live through her problems could be an easy way. There is nothing in our New Testament to imply this. Problems would not be problems if they did not cause trouble and heartache and anxiety. But God knows this too. He does not expect us to sail through, flashing a victorious smile in the face of tragedy and confusion. He does expect us to face facts. ". . . now we see indistinctly in a mirror," Paul also wrote. Mirrors in the days during which the great Apostle was writing threw back distorted images at best. They were made of polished metal and gave a wavy, blurred reflection. The fact is we cannot see or understand everything now, and God knows this. He also knows and longs for us to remember that one day we will be able to see "face to face."

"Now we know partly, but then we shall understand as completely as we are understood."

God understands us. God understands our problems. He knows the innermost twistings in the deepest depths of your personality and that of your loved ones and neighbors. He does not hold out the promise that we will understand fully on this earth, but He does urge us to make the maximum use of the minds and heart-perception He offers us.

One day, one breath-taking day when we stand face to face with Him, we *will* understand as completely as we are understood now.

Until then, He pleads with us to have *faith* in Him, to *hope* because of Him, and to act on the *fact* that the greatest of all these *is* love.

A woman can muddle through her earthly problems, feeling a victim of the circumstances of her life, or she can live through her problems — out of confusion to peace. As I understand this, *living* through our problems means *loving* through.

If we simply stay attached to Christ, the Vine, all the love we need will be supplied to us. Our God cannot be in short supply. He *is* love.

But a woman must choose.